Domestic and Relationship Abuse

Volume 224

Series Editor

Lisa Firth

Independence

Educational Publishers

Cambridge

First published by Independence

The Studio, High Green

Great Shelford

Cambridge CB22 5EG

England

© Independence 2012

British Library Cataloguing in Publication Data

Domestic and relationship abuse. -- (Issues ; v. 224)

1. Family violence.

I. Series II. Firth, Lisa.

362.8'292-dc23

ISBN-13: 978 1 86168 613 8

Printed in Great Britain

MWL Print Group Ltd

CONTENTS

Chapter 1 Domestic Abuse

Chapter 2 Young People and Abuse

Chapter 3 Dealing with Abuse

OTHER TITLES IN THE ISSUES SERIES

For more on these titles, visit: www.independence.co.uk

A note on critical evaluation

Because the information reprinted here is from a number of different sources, readers should bear in mind the origin of the text and whether the source is likely to have a particular bias when presenting information (just as they would if undertaking their own research). It is hoped that, as you read about the many aspects of the issues explored in this book, you will critically evaluate the information presented. It is important that you decide whether you are being presented with facts or opinions. Does the writer give a biased or an unbiased report? If an opinion is being expressed, do you agree with the writer?

Domestic and Relationship Abuse offers a useful starting point for those who need convenient access to information about the many issues involved. However, it is only a starting point. Following each article is a URL to the relevant organisation's website, which you may wish to visit for further information.

Domestic abuse

Within any relationship, there are ups and downs – people say and do things to each other that are hurtful. However, there's a difference between a normal argument and abusive, fighting and threatening behaviour: this is domestic violence or abuse.

What is domestic abuse?

Women's Aid defines domestic abuse as:

'Physical, sexual, psychological or financial violence that takes place within an intimate or family-type relationship and that forms a pattern of coercive and controlling behaviour. This can include forced marriage and so-called "honour crimes". Domestic violence may include a range of abusive behaviours, not all of which are in themselves inherently 'violent'.

The Government defines domestic violence as:

'Any incident of threatening behaviour, violence or abuse (psychological, physical, sexual, financial or emotional) between adults who are or have been intimate partners or family members, regardless of gender or sexuality.' This includes issues of concern to black and minority ethnic (BME) communities such as so-called 'honour killings'.

Types of abuse

Domestic violence is a pattern of abusive behaviour that includes emotional, physical, sexual and financial abuse. It's about using power and control over the other person. Domestic violence generally doesn't happen just once: over time it tends to happen more often and becomes more serious and severe.

Domestic violence doesn't always have to be physical; it often also includes emotional, financial and sexual abuse. Many of these behaviours are crimes. Abuse is not an accident – it is behaviour that is done on purpose to control and intimidate the other person. The impact on the abused person can be devastating – physical injury, psychological injury, depression, living in constant fear, self-harming.

⇨ Physical abuse – e.g. hitting, punching, burning, strangling, slapping, biting, pinching, kicking, pulling hair out, pushing, shoving.

⇨ Sexual abuse – e.g. forcing unwanted sexual acts, including rape; using force, threats or intimidation to make you perform sexual acts; having sex with you when you don't want to have sex; any degrading treatment based on your sexual orientation.

⇨ Emotional abuse – e.g. constant criticism, insults, undermining capabilities.

⇨ Isolation – e.g. preventing someone from having or developing family, social or professional relationships; preventing from working; monitoring or blocking their telephone calls.

⇨ Financial abuse – e.g. withholding money; making a person account for every penny they spend; taking their money without asking.

⇨ Threats – e.g. making angry gestures; using physical size to intimidate; shouting them down; destroying their possessions; breaking things; punching walls; wielding a knife or a gun; threatening to kill or harm their partner and the children.

Domestic abuse is often a combination of several, if not all, of the above.

Is there a reason for violence, like drinking or drugs?

There's never any excuse for violence or abuse.

⇨ All types of abuse are wrong and the victim is never to blame.

⇨ Children and young people are also never to blame for domestic violence that happens between adults. It is not their fault – even if the argument is about them!

⇨ Domestic violence is about power and control. The abuser feels powerful and strong by hurting the other person and making the other person feel frightened or intimidated about themselves.

⇨ Violence is a choice.

⇨ Domestic violence is not caused by drink or drug use. Drinking and drugs can make the abuse worse, but they do not cause the abuse to happen.

⇨ Abusers might say that they are feeling stressed because of money issues or because they don't have a job. Lots of abusers will say they only behave like this because their partner asks for it or deserves it because of something they've done.

WOMEN'S AID

Who does it happen to?

Domestic violence and abuse happens between two people in a family or between two people who are in an intimate relationship with each other. It happens to all people in society regardless of ethnicity, socio-economic status or age. Domestic violence happens within young people's relationships, within gay and lesbian relationships, to disabled people or between family members. More often than not men are the abusers and women are the victims, but domestic violence can also happen to men.

In the year 2006/07 it is estimated that 17,545 women and 25,451 children were accommodated in Women's Aid refuges throughout England

When you look at the roles of men and women in history it can help you to understand why it happens more to women. Historically, women had very few legal rights: they couldn't own property or divorce their husbands; they could only work in certain jobs and were paid much less than men. In many societies, it's been the role of women to mind the home, cook, clean and care for the children and for their husband. Traditionally, it's been the man's role to work and earn the money for the family. Men made the rules and women and children had to follow them. A man had the right to beat his wife and children if he felt they deserved it.

In the UK, a lot has changed since then – things are much better now! In the last century women fought hard to win more rights, such as the right to vote, the right to study and to work. Women now have careers and men and women share the responsibilities of taking care of the home and children.

Men and women should be treated as equals, but this is still not always the case. Many societies and cultures still believe that men are stronger and more powerful than women and this makes some people think that violence between men and women is ok – but it's not! Men and women are still working hard today to change this way of thinking and to stop domestic violence from happening.

Domestic violence can happen to anyone – it doesn't matter what race, ethnicity or religion they are, or how much money they have. It happens to people all over the world.

I've heard it happens more to women – is that true?

⇨ One in four women will experience domestic abuse in their lifetime.

⇨ Domestic abuse currently claims the lives of around two women per week.

⇨ It accounts for 15% of all violent incidents.

Domestic violence can happen to anyone – it doesn't matter what race, ethnicity or religion they are, or how much money they have. It happens to people all over the world

⇨ 89% of those suffering four or more incidents are women.

⇨ There is an incident of domestic abuse reported to the police every minute.

⇨ In the year 2006/07 it is estimated that 17,545 women and 25,451 children were accommodated in Women's Aid refuges throughout England.

⇨ The above information is reprinted from The Hideout with kind permission from the Women's Aid Federation of England. Please visit their website at www.thehideout.org.uk for more information.

© Women's Aid

DAD HIT... ERR... I MEAN, I FELL OVER.

WOMEN'S AID

Types of domestic abuse

There are different types of domestic abuse, including emotional, psychological, physical, sexual and financial abuse. Many abusers behave in ways that include more than one type of domestic violence, and the boundaries between some of these behaviours are often quite blurred.

Emotional or psychological abuse

Emotional or psychological abuse can be verbal or non-verbal. Its aim is to chip away at the confidence and independence of victims with the intention of making them compliant and limiting their ability to leave. Emotional abuse includes verbal abuse such as yelling, name-calling, blaming and shaming, isolation, intimidation, threats of violence and controlling behaviour.

Many abused women define the psychological effects of domestic abuse as having a 'more profound' effect on their lives – even where there has been life-threatening or disabling physical violence. Despite this, there is almost always pressure to define domestic abuse in terms of actual, or threatened, physical violence.

Physical abuse

There are a broad range of behaviours that come under the heading of physical abuse, including actions such as punching, slapping, hitting, biting, pinching, kicking, pulling hair out, pushing, shoving, burning and strangling. It should be noted that strangulation is the most common method of intimate partner homicide.

Sexual abuse

Rape and sexual abuse are common in abusive relationships because a women's right to consent is likely to be ignored. In fact, evidence suggests that 45% of all rape is committed by current partners and these incidents are less likely to come to the attention of the police than those committed by strangers. Any situation in which an individual is forced to participate in unwanted, unsafe or degrading sexual activity is sexual abuse. In addition, women whose partners abuse them physically and sexually are thought to be at a higher risk of experiencing multiple and escalating assaults. Research also indicates that women who are raped by their husbands or partners are likely to suffer severe psychological effects because of the prolonged level of fear they are likely to experience.

Economic or financial abuse

Economic or financial abuse aims to limit a victim's ability to access help. Tactics may include controlling the finances; withholding money or credit cards; making someone unreasonably account for money spent/petrol used; exploiting assets; withholding basic necessities; preventing someone from working; deliberately running up debts; forcing someone to work against their will and sabotaging someone's job.

Honour-based violence

'Honour'-based violence (HBV) is a form of domestic abuse which is perpetrated in the name of so-called 'honour'. The honour code which it refers to is set at the discretion of male relatives and women who do not abide by the 'rules' are then punished for bringing shame on the family. Infringements may include a woman having a boyfriend; rejecting a forced marriage; pregnancy outside of marriage; interfaith relationships; seeking divorce; inappropriate dress or make-up, and even kissing in a public place.

HBV can exist in any culture or community where males are in position to establish and enforce women's conduct. Examples include: Turkish; Kurdish; Afghani; South Asian; African; Middle Eastern; South and Eastern European; Gypsy and the travelling community (this is not an exhaustive list).

Males can also be victims, sometimes as a consequence of a relationship which is deemed to be inappropriate, if they are gay, have a disability or if they have assisted a victim.

This is not a crime which is perpetrated by men only: sometimes female relatives will support, incite or assist. It is also not unusual for younger relatives to be selected to undertake the abuse as a way to protect senior members of the family. Sometimes contract killers and bounty hunters will also be employed.

Forced marriage

A forced marriage is a marriage that is performed under duress and without the full and informed consent or free will of both parties.

Victims of forced marriage may be the subject of physical violence, rape, abduction, false imprisonment, enslavement, emotional abuse and murder. It is important not to confuse forced marriage with arranged marriage. In the instance of an arranged marriage, both parties freely consent.

Female genital mutilation

Female genital mutilation (FGM), sometimes referred to as female circumcision, involves females, usually under the age of 16, undergoing procedures wrongly

NHS BARKING AND DAGENHAM

believed to ensure their chastity and marital fidelity. Health professionals are often best placed to identify women who have experienced FGM.

The procedure can range from impairment to complete removal of the labia and clitoris. This is often done without the young women's consent, anaesthetic or with regard for infection. It is estimated that every year, two million women will undergo genital mutilation.

FGM occurs in parts of Africa, the Middle East, Indonesia, Malaysia, Pakistan and Iraq. Many girls living in Britain will be affected as they are taken from their homes to other countries to undergo this procedure. This practice is against the law under the Female Genital Mutilation Act (2003), even if the procedure is undertaken abroad.

30% of domestic violence starts or worsens during pregnancy

Elder abuse

Domestic abuse can include elder abuse. This is where harm is done, or distress caused, to an older person within a relationship where there is an expectation of trust. Most victims of elder abuse are older women with a chronic illness or disability. Again, the most typical abusers are partners, adult children or family members.

⇨ 500,000 are believed to be abused at any one time in the UK.

⇨ Half of the people who abuse are related to the person they are abusing, but very rarely (in only 1% of cases) is the abuser the main family carer.

⇨ 53% of those who abuse are sons or daughters.

⇨ Those between 80 to 89 years old are the most vulnerable to abuse.

⇨ Two-thirds of abuse is committed at home, by someone in a position of trust.

⇨ In 37% of situations, two types of abuse occur simultaneously.

⇨ In a third of circumstances, the abuse is perpetrated by more than one person in collusion.

Domestic abuse perpetrated against people with disabilities

Research commissioned by Women's Aid in October 2007 reveals that people with disabilities are more vulnerable to domestic violence and will often face additional difficulties in attempting to access support. It included the following findings:

⇨ 50% of disabled women have experienced domestic abuse compared with 25% of non-disabled women.

⇨ Disabled women are twice as likely to be assaulted or raped as non-disabled women.

⇨ Both men and women with a limiting illness or disabilities are more likely to experience intimate partner violence.

⇨ Disabled women are likely to have to endure it for longer because appropriate support is not available.

⇨ A study of women who access mental health services identified between 50% and 60% had experienced domestic violence, and up to 20% were currently being abused.

Teen 'dating' abuse

Domestic abuse is not limited to adults; there is an increasing awareness of domestic violence within teen relationships.

⇨ One in five teenage girls have been assaulted by a boyfriend.

⇨ Young women are more likely to experience sexual violence than other age groups.

⇨ Young women with older partners are at increased risk of victimisation.

⇨ Recent surveys (including Zero Tolerance and End Violence Against Women campaign) reveal that approximately 40% of our young people are already being subjected to relationship abuse in their teenage years.

Domestic abuse during pregnancy

Domestic abuse during pregnancy is a major public health concern, with serious consequences for maternal and infant health. The *British Journal of Obstetrics and Gynaecology* reports that one in six pregnant women will experience domestic violence. Evidence also suggests that around 30% of domestic violence starts or worsens during pregnancy. Where abuse occurs during pregnancy, injury to the abdomen, breasts and genitals are common. It follows that domestic abuse is a factor in a significant proportion of maternal and perinatal mortality and morbidity.

Commonly, violence during pregnancy can cause placental separation, foetal fractures, antepartum haemorrhage, rupture of the uterus and pre-term labour. Abuse can also indirectly impact upon the health of a woman and her baby through poor diet and restricted access to antenatal care.

In 2000, the Department of Health endorsed routine antenatal enquiry for domestic violence: this was also

endorsed by the Royal College of Obstetricians and Gynaecologists, the Royal College of Midwives and NICE, who in 2001 recommended that all pregnant women should be asked routinely about domestic abuse as part of their social history.

Domestic abuse within gay, lesbian, bisexual and transgender relationships

Domestic abuse can happen to anyone regardless of whether they are heterosexual, gay, lesbian, bisexual or transgender.

Every individual's experience of domestic abuse will be unique. However, gay, lesbian, bisexual and transgender individuals are likely to face additional concerns around homophobia and gender discrimination. They may also be concerned that they will not be recognised as victims or believed and taken seriously. Abusers may also be able to control their victims through the threat of 'outing'.

Domestic abuse against men

Domestic abuse is often talked about in a gendered manner, but it is important to recognise that men experience domestic abuse as victims too. Men's experiences are likely to be significantly different to women's though.

It is important to recognise that men experience domestic abuse as victims too

The research that is available suggests that women are more likely than men to experience domestic abuse in their lives and to suffer repeated victimisation. They are also more likely to be injured, or have to seek medical help. Another difference is that men are less likely to be murdered by female abusers; Home Office figures reveal that on average, 100 women a year and around 30 men a year are killed within a domestic abuse context. Women are almost exclusively killed by men, whereas in contrast, approximately one-third of the men are killed by other men and a little under a third are killed by women against whom they have a documented history of abuse.

Many men who experience domestic abuse from a current or former partner find it difficult to get support, not least because it can be hard for men to acknowledge and discuss their experiences. This can be due to any number of reasons, including love for a partner, embarrassment or shame and concern for any children, or simply not knowing where to go.

Men may attempt different techniques to cope. Coping strategies can include adopting an 'I can handle this' attitude and adapting their behaviour to appease the abuser. Coping strategies like this may make life temporarily safer and easier but they are unlikely to stop the abuse.

All statutory agencies have a responsibility to support male victims of domestic violence. The national help-line for male victims of domestic violence is a good starting point – the Men's Advice Line: 0808 801 0327.

Stalking

While stalking may be perpetrated by strangers or acquaintances, stalking is most often committed against women by former or current partners. Any allegation of stalking should be taken very seriously as it is synonymous with an increased risk of serious harm or murder. (Stalking was a feature in 40% of those domestic murders reviewed by the Metropolitan Police and has also been especially identified as a shared feature of murders where there have not been previously recorded incidents of violence.)

⇨ Information from NHS Barking and Dagenham. Please visit the Domestic Violence London website at www.domesticviolencelondon.nhs.uk for more information on this and other related topics.

© NHS Barking and Dagenham 2012

No... We're happily married!

NHS BARKING AND DAGENHAM

Myths of domestic violence

There are many myths surrounding domestic violence. By believing them we allow the problem to continue.

Refuge
For women and children.
Against domestic violence.

Myth: Alcohol and drugs make men violent

Many men are violent when stone-cold sober. Others never touch alcohol, yet regularly abuse their partner.

Blaming drink or drugs is an excuse, a way of denying responsibility. Both may be the trigger for a particular attack, but they are not the cause.

Myth: It only happens in poor families on council estates

Anyone can be abused, no matter where they live or how much income they have. Abused women come from all walks of life and there are no exceptions. You only have to think of the celebrities we hear about in the papers to realise that money cannot protect you from domestic violence.

Men who abuse women are as likely to be lawyers, accountants and judges as they are milkmen, cleaners or unemployed.

Women from different cultures can find it difficult to leave an abusive man, as this would bring shame on both themselves and their family

Myth: More women would leave if the abuse was that bad

There are many reasons for staying with an abusive partner. The abused woman may fear what her partner will do if she leaves, or she may believe that staying with him is better for the children.

There are also practical considerations to take into account. She may not have access to money, or anywhere to go. She may not know where to turn for help, particularly if English is not her first language. And when she is emotionally and financially dependent on her partner she can be very isolated.

Women from different cultures can find it particularly difficult to leave an abusive man, as this would bring shame on both themselves and their family. They may feel they are betraying their community if they contact the police.

An abused woman's self-esteem will have been steadily worn down. She may not believe she will manage on her own, or that she has any other options. She may have been brainwashed into thinking she's worthless. She will feel ashamed of what has happened and perhaps convinced it is her fault.

She hopes her partner will change. She remembers the good times at the start of the relationship and hopes they will return. In emotional terms she has made a huge investment in the relationship and she wants it to work.

Myth: Abusers grow up in violent homes

This is not true. Growing up in a violent home is a risk factor and some children who experience abuse do go on to be abusive in their relationships. On the other hand, many do not. Instead they are repelled by violence as adults because they have seen the damage it causes – they would not dream of hitting their partner.

Abusers learn to be violent from the society they grow up in. Inequality between the sexes means that men have more power over women – inevitably some of them abuse or exploit that power.

People who blame violence on their childhood experiences avoid taking responsibility for their actions. Violence is a choice an abuser makes.

Myth: Some women like violence

Women do not enjoy violence, or find it a turn-on. Most live in fear and terror. This is a way of blaming the victim for what is happening.

Myth: Women ask for it. They deserve what they get

Women are often attacked by their partner for no apparent reason. Even if a woman has behaved appallingly, she does not deserve to be beaten. Violence and intimidation are not acceptable ways to solve conflict in a relationship.

Again, this is a way of justifying and making excuses for the abuser's behaviour. It allows a violent man to avoid responsibility for his actions.

REFUGE

Myth: Abusive men have a mental illness

The vast majority of men who abuse are not mentally ill. Research shows that the proportion of abusers with mental health problems is no higher than in society as a whole. And if an abusive man were mentally ill, how is it that he only abuses his partner, not his colleagues, strangers or friends?

Myth: He only hit her because he was under stress

Some men who abuse their partners are suffering from stress. Again, this is a factor, not a cause. Many men who are stressed are never abusive. Similarly, many men who do abuse their partner cannot claim to be under stress.

Women experience stress too, yet they rarely beat or abuse their partners to the extent that men abuse women.

Myth: He loses his temper sometimes, that's all

People argue that an abusive man loses his temper, or is out of control. In fact he is very much in control.

Abusers can be selective about when they hit their partner, e.g when the children are asleep. Or choose not to mark her face, or any part of the body which

shows. This suggests they are very aware of what they are doing. Many men abuse their partners emotionally and psychologically, without ever using anger or physical violence. This shows the extent of their control.

Myth: Domestic violence is a private matter, you shouldn't get involved

For too long domestic violence has been allowed to happen behind closed doors. People think what goes on in the home is private, and not their problem.

People argue that an abusive man loses his temper, or is out of control. In fact he is very much in control

---

Domestic violence is a crime. It is against the law.

We are all affected by domestic violence, and we all have a responsibility to speak out against it. Only then will we end it.

⇨ The above information is reprinted with kind permission from Refuge. Visit www.refuge.org.uk for more information.

© Refuge

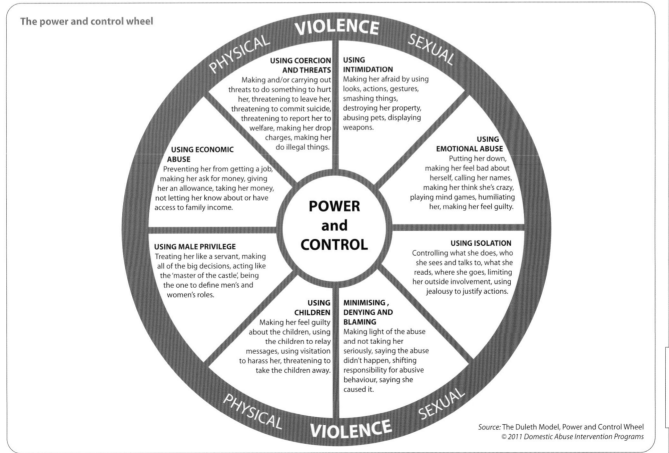

The power and control wheel

VIOLENCE

PHYSICAL — SEXUAL

USING COERCION AND THREATS
Making and/or carrying out threats to do something to hurt her, threatening to leave her, threatening to commit suicide, threatening to report her to welfare, making her drop charges, making her do illegal things.

USING INTIMIDATION
Making her afraid by using looks, actions, gestures, smashing things, destroying her property, abusing pets, displaying weapons.

USING EMOTIONAL ABUSE
Putting her down, making her feel bad about herself, calling her names, making her think she's crazy, playing mind games, humiliating her, making her feel guilty.

USING ECONOMIC ABUSE
Preventing her from getting a job, making her ask for money, giving her an allowance, taking her money, not letting her know about or have access to family income.

POWER and CONTROL

USING MALE PRIVILEGE
Treating her like a servant, making all of the big decisions, acting like the 'master of the castle', being the one to define men's and women's roles.

USING ISOLATION
Controlling what she does, who she sees and talks to, what she reads, where she goes, limiting her outside involvement, using jealousy to justify actions.

USING CHILDREN
Making her feel guilty about the children, using the children to relay messages, using visitation to harass her, threatening to take the children away.

MINIMISING, DENYING AND BLAMING
Making light of the abuse and not taking her seriously, saying the abuse didn't happen, shifting responsibility for abusive behaviour, saying she caused it.

PHYSICAL — SEXUAL

VIOLENCE

Source: The Duleth Model, Power and Control Wheel
© 2011 Domestic Abuse Intervention Programs

REFUGE

Paula's story

Information from Refuge.

**For women and children.
Against domestic violence.**

I met Jason when I was in my early 30s. What attracted me to him was how charming he was. He was really nice to me. But now, looking back, I can see that all of the signs were there.

He began to get more and more controlling. He would call me all the time and if I wanted to see my friends he would start an argument so I wouldn't go. When my friends came over he was rude to them – he even threw one of them out of the house. If I was on the phone to someone he'd be shouting in the background.

He started to put me down all the time. He would criticise everything about me – my clothes, my friends, my weight. I become so timid. He could manipulate me so easily – I lost all my confidence. It started to affect my work, I lost so many of my friends. I wasn't happy any more.

After we got married we moved to a new town and I thought it would be a new start and things would change, but they just got worse. A month after the wedding he hit me for the first time – so hard I had to go to hospital. He had just got home from work and he flew into a rage because dinner wasn't ready. He punched me in the face so many times that I needed 23 stitches. I had to beg him to let me to go to hospital and when we got there he didn't leave me alone for a second. He told me that if I told anyone what happened he would kill me. So I had to say I hit my face on a cupboard door.

After that the beatings just got worse. He used to lock the doors and take my keys and phone, so I couldn't get away. People at work saw when he had beaten me up, but no-one ever asked me what was going on. Gradually I started to believe him when he said the abuse was my fault.

We decided to go away for a weekend and I thought that might help things. But on the first night he started an argument over nothing and he just went wild. I ran downstairs and got the hotel staff to call the police. I was a total mess – he had broken three ribs and my face was completely swollen with bruises. He was arrested and sent to prison for 13 weeks. When he was released he tracked me down and attacked me in the street. He was sent back to prison for another 13 weeks and the police suggested that I get in touch with Refuge and move away from the area.

Refuge found me a place in a new town before he was released again. When I arrived I was in shock. It was difficult adapting to a new place, but I can't describe how it felt to be safe and free. The Refuge staff gave me lots of emotional support, and it was really helpful to be able to meet the other women in the refuge who had been through the same things as me.

> *He would criticise everything about me – my clothes, my friends, my weight. I become so timid. He could manipulate me so easily – I lost all my confidence*

The staff helped me access the benefits I needed to stay in the refuge and, when I was ready, helped me to find a new, safe place to live. They even helped me get on to training courses in the area so I could rebuild my career.

Things are really good now. I have my own flat, I'm back at work, I go out with my friends – I feel so much more confident. Now I can come home and feel safe. There's no fear about what's going to happen. Contacting Refuge was the best thing I've ever done. They helped me with so much. If it wasn't for them I'd still be in that house.

⇨ Information from Refuge. Visit www.refuge.org.uk for more.

REFUGE

The invisible domestic violence – against men

More women are being convicted of domestic violence, but discovering the true number of male victims is a complex affair.

By Nicola Graham-Kevan

That women accounted for 7% of all convictions for domestic violence last year will come as a surprise to many. But what is not clear is whether the growing numbers of women convicted – a 150% increase in five years – represents a rise in actual cases of female-perpetrated domestic violence.

Domestic violence has traditionally been understood as a crime perpetrated by domineering men against defenceless women. Research spanning over 40 years has, however, consistently found that men and women self-report perpetrating domestic violence at similar rates. Professor John Archer from the University of Central Lancashire has conducted a number of meta-analytic reviews of these studies and found that women are as likely to use domestic violence as men, but women are twice as likely as men to be injured or killed during a domestic assault. Men still represent a substantial proportion of people who are assaulted, injured or killed by an intimate partner (50%, 30% and 25%, respectively).

Why has women's domestic violence towards men been unreported for so long, and what has changed in the last five years to make it more visible?

If the empirical research is correct in suggesting that between a quarter and half of all domestic violence victims are men, a question follows: why has women's domestic violence towards men been unreported for so long, and what has changed in the last five years to make it more visible?

One reason may be the feminist movement. Feminism took up the cause of the domestic abuse of women in the 1970s, with the world's first women's refuge being opened by Erin Pizzey in 1971. Feminism understood domestic violence as the natural extension of men's patriarchal attitudes towards women, leading men to feel they had the right to control their partners, using violence if necessary. Feminists campaigned successfully to bring the issue into the public arena, thereby securing resources to establish services to help victims. This activism and advocacy led to governmental and public acceptance that 'domestic violence' was synonymous with violence against women.

Paradoxically, feminist concerns for female victims may also have led to the recent increase in arrests of female perpetrators. The disparity between prevalence study statistics and criminal conviction data of male domestic violence perpetration led US feminists to successfully campaign for mandatory arrest policies for domestic violence call-outs. Mandatory arrest policies coincided with a three-fold increase in the number of women arrested. In the UK, a pro-arrest policy was also introduced, requiring police forces to always consider an arrest in domestic violence cases. Although not eliminating police discretion, the policy undoubtedly diminished individual police officers' discretionary powers. The increase in female arrests for domestic violence suggests that when police officers were freer to exercise discretion, it was exercised more frequently in favour of female perpetrators.

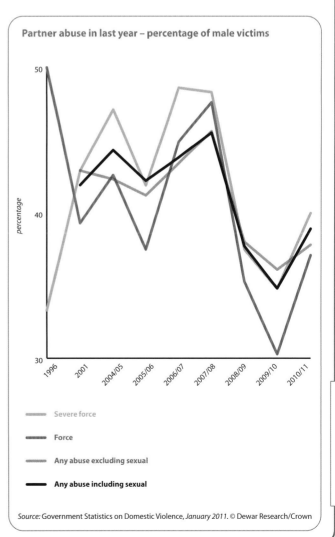

Partner abuse in last year – percentage of male victims

Severe force

Force

Any abuse excluding sexual

Any abuse including sexual

Source: Government Statistics on Domestic Violence, *January 2011.* © Dewar Research/Crown

THE GUARDIAN

Support for a feminist conceptualisation of domestic violence has been afforded by men's generally more visible violent behaviour. Men make up the majority of perpetrators of violence in public places, such as football matches and nightclubs. As men appear to be more ready, willing and able to use violence outside the home, the logical extension is that men are more violent than women *per se*. This argument has frequently been cited by researchers such as Professors Russell and Emerson Dobash as evidence against the veracity of figures showing large numbers of male victims of domestic violence, while ignoring the fact that men's aggression in public places is almost always directed towards other men.

Men make up the majority of perpetrators of violence in public places, such as football matches and nightclubs

In recent years, female violence has become a more public affair, with changes in drinking patterns being a likely contributing factor to more women being arrested for violent offences outside of the home. In addition, the widespread use of CCTV may have provided sufficient evidence for the police and CPS to override stereotypes of women as non-violent. The erosion of the passive female stereotype is likely to result in more women being charged and convicted of offences generally, which might also result in increases in the conviction rates for women's domestic violence.

If current trends continue ... men [will be] more likely to be offered help and protection

The dual stereotypes of the violent man and passive woman have undoubtedly obscured the existence of male victims of domestic violence in the past. Men were also unlikely to view their own victimisation as either domestic violence or a criminal assault, and so were unlikely to seek help.

Large sums of money have been spent on educational campaigns to encourage female victims to seek help. Until there are similar campaigns for men, it is unlikely that the true number of male victims needing help will be known. If the current trends continue, however, women may find themselves increasingly likely to be charged with domestic assault, and men more likely to be offered help and protection.

7 June 2011

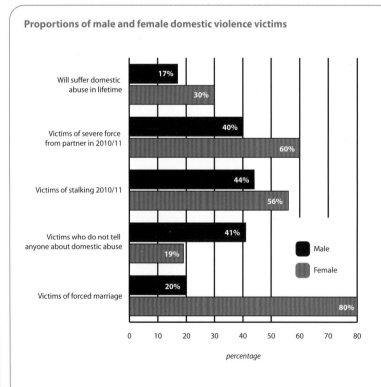

Proportions of male and female domestic violence victims

- Will suffer domestic abuse in lifetime — Male 17%, Female 30%
- Victims of severe force from partner in 2010/11 — Male 40%, Female 60%
- Victims of stalking 2010/11 — Male 44%, Female 56%
- Victims who do not tell anyone about domestic abuse — Male 41%, Female 19%
- Victims of forced marriage — Male 20%, Female 80%

Male / Female

percentage

Refuge spaces available in the UK for male and female domestic abuse victims

Spaces available for female abuse victims 7,500

Spaces available for male abuse victims 72

Source: Male victims of domestic and partner abuse, 15 key facts, October 2011. ManKind Initiative.

THE GUARDIAN

Male victims of domestic and partner abuse

Key facts from the ManKind Initiative.

⇨ For every three victims of partner abuse, two will be female, one will be male.

⇨ One in six (17%) men (aged 16 or over) and one in four women (30%) will suffer domestic abuse in their lifetime. This equates to around 2.6 million men and around 4.5 million women. 5% of men and 7% of women were victims in 2010/11, a ratio of 42% men and 58% women.

⇨ In terms of partner abuse, 3.7% of men and 5.8% of women stated they had been a victim in 2010/11, with 1.0% of men and 1.5% of women stating they were a victim of severe force from their partner – 40% men and 60% women.

⇨ 44% of stalking victims in 2010/11 were male.

⇨ 21 men and 95 women were murdered by a partner/ ex-partner (classified as the key suspect) in 2009/10. This equates to one man every 17 days.

⇨ The most prevalent age group for male victims is 25–34, where 3.7% of men stated they were a victim of partner abuse, compared to 1.7% of 45- to 54-year-old men. 3.6% of 16- to 19-year-old men and 3.0% of 20- to 24-year-old men said they had also been a victim.

⇨ Married men (1.5%) are less likely to be a victim of partner abuse than cohabiting men (3.5%) and single men (3.2%) who have a girlfriend/boyfriend but are not living with them.

⇨ The number of gay or bisexual men who suffered partner abuse in 2008/09 (6.2%) is nearly double the number for heterosexual men (3.3%).

⇨ 20% of men who have suffered partner abuse have done so for more than one year (97,000 men).

⇨ The number of women convicted of perpetrating domestic abuse has risen five-fold in the past seven years, from 806 (2004/05) to 3,965 (2010/11).

⇨ Twice as many male victims (41%) as female (19%) do not tell anyone about the domestic abuse they are suffering, highlighting the level of underreporting.

⇨ 20% of forced marriage victims are men.

⇨ The average male victim is 43, is 5ft 9in tall and weighs 13st. The average female perpetrator is 40, is 5ft 4in tall and weighs 10st 7lb.

⇨ There are 72 bed spaces in 20 refuges or safe houses available to male victims in the UK, run by ten organisations. Of these, 44 spaces are also available to female victims and 18 are exclusively for gay men. There are over an estimated 400 organisations, with 500 refuges (with 7,500 spaces) in the UK specifically for women.

⇨ In 2010, on 17 occasions we tried to find a refuge or safe house place for a male victim but found that the few places available were all full.

⇨ The biggest problem, though, is that there are no places at all available in a man's local community. On at least 120 occasions in 2010, a caller decided not to consider a refuge or safe house because they were too far away and would mean having to completely uproot their lives.

⇨ The number of calls to the ManKind Initiative's helpline from victims or people (normally mothers or sisters) calling on behalf of victims increased by 35% between 2009 and 2010.

October 2011

⇨ The above information is reproduced with kind permission from the ManKind Initiative. Sources can be viewed at www.mankind.org.uk

© *ManKind*

MANKIND

Understanding LGBT domestic abuse

Understanding the myths and the actual reality of domestic abuse in LGBT relationships is critical if we are to respond to victims and perpetrators effectively.

There are a number of myths about domestic abuse in LGBT (lesbian, gay, bisexual and transgender) relationships that can prevent people seeking help. Sometimes an abuser will deliberately use these myths to try and stop the victim reporting their experiences.

In the case of domestic abuse in LGBT relationships, myths are often based on prejudice or stereotypical attitudes towards LGBT relationships

In the case of domestic abuse in LGBT relationships, myths are often based on prejudice or stereotypical attitudes towards LGBT relationships. As a result, they divert attention away from the actions of the abuser.

Here are examples of common myths surrounding LGBT domestic abuse:

Myth: Domestic abuse doesn't happen in LGBT relationships

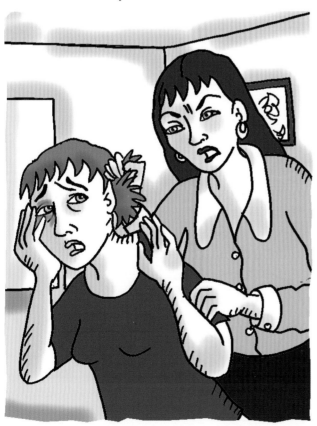

Reality: Recent research suggests that domestic abuse is a significant issue in LGBT relationships. Some research suggests that around one in four LGBT people will experience domestic abuse at some point in their lives. This is the same as the number of straight women who will experience domestic abuse in their lifetime.

Myth: Any abuse in LGBT intimate relationships is mutual so both partners are equally responsible for it

Reality: Abuse is a systematic pattern of behaviour used by one person in a relationship to gain power and control over their partner. In some circumstances the abuser may physically hurt their partner, and the partner may defend themselves. However, this is not a mutual fight, but self-defence.

Abuse is not about physical strength and it crosses all boundaries of physical size and appearance

Emotional abuse, which is another way to control the abused partner, can often cause more long-lasting harm than physical abuse. It is never acceptable for anyone to live in fear of their partner.

Myth: The victim and perpetrator can be identified by their physical appearance, e.g. the abuser will be butch and the victim will be more feminine, the perpetrator will be older or bigger and the victim younger or smaller

Reality: Abuse is not about physical strength and it crosses all boundaries of physical size and appearance. The power of one person over another does not come from physical strength but from manipulative controlling behaviour and can include emotional abuse.

Myth: Abuse is a 'normal' part of LGBT relationships caused by the 'fact' that there is something inherently wrong with LGBT relationships

Reality: It is not true that domestic abuse is a 'normal' part of LGBT relationships. The idea of abuse as normal, however, can be used as a powerful tool by a

VICTIM SUPPORT

perpetrator, particularly when a victim is younger or less experienced.

Some research suggests that around one in four LGBT people will experience domestic abuse at some point in their lives. This is the same as the number of straight women who will experience domestic abuse in their lifetime

Myth: It is easier for LGBT people to leave an abusive relationship as they have fewer ties, e.g. they do not have children, or where the victim is not the 'real' or biological parent

Reality: For LGBT people there are some specific circumstances that can make it even more difficult for them to leave an abuser. LGBT people may be isolated from family because of discrimination in relation to their sexual orientation or gender identity and so may not be able to draw on family support, even at the beginning of a relationship. If it is a first-time same-sex relationship for one partner there may be a huge amount of emotional investment in it.

Research demonstrates that LGBT people can be reluctant to turn to mainstream services because of fears of homophobia or of being 'outed' or of an inappropriate response. They may be fearful of leaving because the abuser has threatened to 'out' them if they do leave. Research also highlights that because domestic abuse is often seen as something which heterosexual women experience, some LGBT people may not actually realise that what they are experiencing is domestic abuse.

Many LGBT people have children and children are affected by abuse in the household. Not being a biological parent does not lessen ties, love or a sense of responsibility.

Myth: The law does not protect LGBT people

Reality: Since 2004 people in LGBT relationships suffering domestic abuse have been equally protected under the law in England, giving them the same legal rights as domestic violence victims in heterosexual relationships. This myth again can be a powerful tool for a perpetrator to persuade the victim they will not be able to access help.

⇨ The above information is reprinted with kind permission from Victim Support. Visit their website at www.victimsupport.com for more information.

© Victim Support

Out of sight, out of mind: transgender people's experience of domestic abuse

Key Findings from LGBT Youth Scotland and the Equality Network's 2010 examination of transgender people's experience of domestic abuse in Scotland.

⇨ 80% of respondents stated that they had experienced emotionally, sexually, or physically abusive behaviour by a partner or ex-partner.

⇨ Although 80% of respondents identified having experienced some form of abusive behaviour from a partner or ex-partner, only 60% of respondents recognised the behaviour as domestic abuse.

⇨ The type of domestic abuse most frequently experienced by the respondents was transphobic emotional abuse, with 73% of the respondents experiencing at least one type of transphobic emotionally abusive behaviour from a partner or ex-partner.

⇨ 60% of respondents had experienced controlling behaviour from a partner or ex-partner.

⇨ 45% of respondents had experienced physically abusive behaviour from a partner or ex-partner.

⇨ 47% of respondents had experienced some form of sexual abuse from a partner or ex-partner.

⇨ 37% of respondents said that someone had forced, or tried to force, them to have sex when they were under the age of 16.

⇨ 46% of respondents said that someone had forced, or tried to force, them to engage in some other form of sexual activity when under the age of 16.

⇨ 10% of respondents stated that someone had forced, or tried to force, them to engage in sexual activity for money.

August 2010

⇨ Information from Victim Support. Please visit www.victimsupport.com for more information.

© Victim Support

What is forced marriage?

Information from ForcedMarriage.net

A forced marriage takes place when the bride, groom or both do not want to get married but are forced to by others, usually their families. People forced into marriage may be tricked into going abroad, physically threatened and/or emotionally blackmailed to do so.

Every year, hundreds of young people in Britain, both male and female, are forced into marriage against their will, often by violence and blackmail from their own families and relatives.

It is a violation of fundamental human rights

Forced marriage is wrong and cannot be justified on any religious or cultural basis. In the UK, forced marriage amounts to a form of domestic violence and/or child abuse. It can affect women and men as well as girls and boys from any community and background.

The British courts have the power to stop someone from forcing someone else to marry against their will

It is different from an arranged marriage

Unlike forced marriages, in an arranged marriage both the bride and groom choose whether or not they want to marry the person suggested to them by their families. In a forced marriage there is no freedom of choice.

It is traumatic and can ruin people's lives

Feeling that they no longer have control over their own lives, many individuals end up depressed, self-harming or, in the worst cases, even attempting suicide.

Living a life you don't want can often seem worse than not living at all.

What happens?

Many families believe that they can only be 'honourable' if their children marry into a particular family or community. They make arrangements for who their child will marry, giving that child absolutely no choice. Often, the victim has never seen, met or spoken to the person they are forced to marry. Homosexuality is often unaccepted too, and on finding out their child is lesbian or gay, a family might force them into a heterosexual marriage against their will.

Emotional blackmail is extremely common

Families often pressurise the victim by saying that they will bring shame on the family if they do not go ahead with the marriage. In many cases, the family threatens to disown the victim, to reject them completely, leaving them with no parents, nowhere to live and unable to contact their own brothers and sisters. Many people are so frightened of being alone in the world and of going against their family's wishes that they feel they cannot escape the marriage, that their only option is to go ahead with it.

The Forced Marriage Unit deals with about 400 cases every year – many of them involving minors

Victims might also be told that to refuse to marry is to go against their religion.

What if you refuse to accept your families' wishes?

Victims may be taken prisoner in their own home. Many who are still at school miss vital parts of their education, as their families fear that if they go to school they might tell other people or run away from the marriage. Often, violence is used on a victim who refuses to go ahead with a marriage, and in the very worst cases, they are murdered.

In some situations, victims are taken to another country and forced into marriage while they are away. Usually they are tricked into going abroad, told that they are going on holiday or to meet relatives, and have no idea about the marriage until they arrive in an unfamiliar country. Without their usual support networks around them (friends, teachers) it's even harder to go against the emotional pressure of their family. Sometimes they have no access to money, their ticket or passport and have no one they can talk to about their situation.

How the law can help

The British courts have the power to stop someone from forcing someone else to marry against their will. An Act of Parliament called the Forced Marriage

FORCEDMARRIAGE.NET

(Civil Protection) Act 2007 provides the courts with powers to make Forced Marriage Protection Orders to stop somebody from forcing another person into marriage. The law also allows the courts to protect victims who have already been forced into marriage, and help them get out of that situation.

A criminal offence?

There is no specific criminal offence of 'forcing someone to marry' within England and Wales. There are, however, several actions that may happen in the process of forcing someone to marry which are criminal offences, such as:

⇨ Assault: trying to harm someone physically.

⇨ Abduction: taking a person away illegally by lying to them or by violence.

⇨ Kidnap: taking a person away illegally by force, against that person's will.

⇨ Imprisonment: keeping a person somewhere against their will.

⇨ Rape: having sex with someone against their will.

⇨ Murder: deliberately killing someone.

Unlike forced marriages, in an arranged marriage both the bride and groom choose whether or not they want to marry the person suggested to them by their families

People who commit these crimes – even if they are relatives of the victim – could be prosecuted.

Did you know?

⇨ Hundreds of young people, particularly girls and young women – some as young as 13 years old – are forced into marriage each year in Britain. Some are taken overseas to marry whilst others may be forced to marry in the UK.

⇨ The Forced Marriage Unit (FMU) deals with about 400 cases every year – many of them involving minors.

⇨ Boys and young men are also victims of forced marriage. About 15 per cent of the FMU's cases involve boys and/or young men being forced to marry against their wishes.

⇨ Forced marriage is not the same as an arranged marriage, in which both spouses can choose whether or not to accept the arrangement. In a forced marriage, one or both spouses do not consent to the marriage or consent is extracted under duress, including physical and emotional pressure.

⇨ Forced marriage can involve child abuse, including abduction, violence, rape, enforced pregnancy and enforced abortion.

⇨ Refusing to marry can place a young person at risk of murder, sometimes also known as 'honour killing'.

⇨ Forced marriage is not sanctioned within any culture or religion.

⇨ The majority of cases in the UK involve South Asian families, but also families from East Asia, the Middle East, Europe and Africa.

⇨ The above information is reproduced with kind permission from ForcedMarriage.net.

© ForcedMarriage.net

Yasmin's story

'I was under a lot of pressure to do the "right thing". My mother and my family used my faith against me – they knew that if I took an oath on the Qur'an, I would keep it. All that mattered to them was what people thought.'

Yasmin was 20 years old when she went to Pakistan with her mother during her university holidays. Yasmin had told her mother that she was a lesbian. On arrival, she was locked in a room and told that she would have to marry her cousin.

Despite attempts to escape, she was kept locked up for a month, and gained her freedom only after she took an oath on the Qur'an that she would agree to marry someone in the UK, which she did on her return. Later, when Yasmin left the marriage, she was disowned by her family. Her ex-husband went on to blackmail Yasmin and her mother.

Had Yasmin known about the support and help that the Forced Marriage Unit can offer, she may have been able to get help sooner and avoid the emotional confusion of forced marriage and divorce. Today, Yasmin has re-established a relationship with her mother and completed her studies.

⇨ Information from ForcedMarriage.net.

© ForcedMarriage.net

FORCEDMARRIAGE.NET

What is teenage relationship abuse?

Information from Home Office.

Research has shown that some teenagers have worryingly high levels of acceptance of abuse within relationships and often justify the abuse with the actions of the victim, e.g. because they were unfaithful.

Several independent studies have shown that 40% of teenagers are in abusive dating relationships

A recent study by the NSPCC and the University of Bristol questioned 1,353 young people (aged between 13 and 17 years old, from eight UK schools) on violence in their intimate relationships.

Why is teenage relationship abuse a hidden problem?

Teenagers experience as much relationship abuse as adults. Several independent studies have shown that 40% of teenagers are in abusive dating relationships. Domestic violence is still a 'hidden' issue in our society; and it is even more so for teenagers. This is exacerbated by the fact that adolescents can be more accepting of, and dismissive about, this form of behaviour than adults.

> 'And he raised his fist to hit me ... and at one point I know it sounds stupid but I wanted him to, because I felt, I felt as if I deserved it, but I was, I was scared.'

The lack of awareness around this issue can be explained, to some extent, by the following factors:

⇨ Teenage romantic relationships can often be short-lived but they are experienced as intensely as adult relationships. Unfortunately, parents and professionals do not always take these relationships seriously enough.

⇨ Adolescents can be more susceptible to gender role stereotypes and can be confused about what their role is within society.

⇨ Because of a lack of experience in constructing respectful relationships and because of their peer group norms it can be difficult for teenagers to judge their partner's behaviour as being abusive.

⇨ Teenage relationship abuse is influenced by how teenagers look at themselves and others. This can be influenced by the media and its portrayal of how we should look and behave.

⇨ First relationships are daunting enough, yet this can be even more difficult if someone is entering into a same-sex relationship and does not feel ready to tell people yet.

⇨ If the young person attends the same school, college or youth club as their abuser, this can increase their sense of fear and entrapment.

Look out for warning signs of relationship abuse. Some of the signs opposite could indicate that a young person is experiencing relationship abuse. This list is not exhaustive and young people respond differently. These signs could also be due to other causes, but it is useful to be aware of common responses.

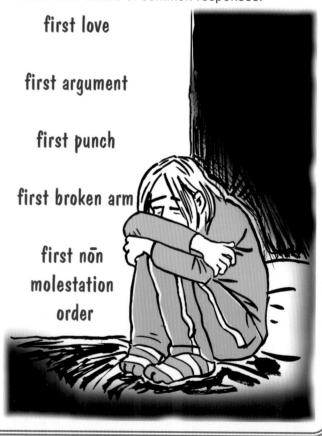

first love

first argument

first punch

first broken arm

first nōn molestation order

HOME OFFICE

- ⇨ Physical signs of injury/illness.
- ⇨ Truancy, failing grades.
- ⇨ Withdrawal, passivity, being compliant.
- ⇨ Changes in mood and personality.
- ⇨ Isolation from family and friends.
- ⇨ Frequent texts and calls from boyfriend/girlfriend.
- ⇨ Inappropriate sexual behaviour/language/attitudes.
- ⇨ Depression.
- ⇨ Pregnancy.
- ⇨ Use of drugs/alcohol (where there was no prior use).
- ⇨ Self-harm.
- ⇨ Eating disorders or problems sleeping.
- ⇨ Symptoms of post-traumatic stress .
- ⇨ Bullying/being bullied.

Impact on education

Relationship abuse can have a negative impact on a young person's cognitive ability which can affect how they behave at school. Signs can include:

- ⇨ Being late for school/not attending (especially if abuser attends same school).

- ⇨ Arriving early/staying late to avoid abuser.
- ⇨ Disturbed sleep affecting concentration.
- ⇨ Not focused in lessons as he or she is preoccupied and worried.
- ⇨ Very gendered expectations of career and achievement.

Relationship abuse can have a negative impact on a young person's cognitive ability which can affect how they behave at school

- ⇨ Feeling unsafe as afraid of being traced by abuser via school.
- ⇨ Appearing isolated and removed.
- ⇨ Worried that everyone at school knows what is happening.

⇨ The above information is an extract from the Home Office document *Teenage Relationship Abuse: A Teacher's Guide to Violence and Abuse in Teenage Relationships*, and is reprinted with permission. Visit www.homeoffice.gov.uk for more information.

© Crown copyright

Key facts and statistics

Information from the Home Office document Teenage Relationship Abuse: A Teacher's Guide to Violence and Abuse in Teenage Relationships.

- ⇨ 33% of girls and 16% of boys reported some form of sexual abuse.
- ⇨ 25% of girls (the same proportion as adult women) and 18% of boys reported some form of physical relationship abuse.
- ⇨ Around 75% of girls and 50% of boys reported some form of emotional relationship abuse.
- ⇨ Most commonly reported forms of emotional abuse, irrespective of gender, were 'being made fun of' and 'constantly being checked up on by a partner'.
- ⇨ Girls were more likely than boys to say that the abuse was repeated and that it either remained at the same level of severity, or worsened, especially after the end of the relationship.
- ⇨ Younger participants (aged 13 to 15 years old) were as likely as older adolescents (aged 16 and over) to experience some forms of relationship abuse.

- ⇨ The majority of young people either told a friend or no-one about the violence; only a minority informed an adult.
- ⇨ Risk factors which may increase a teenager's susceptibility to relationship abuse can include previous experiences of parental domestic violence, physical and sexual abuse and violent peer groups.
- ⇨ Teen relationship abuse can have serious outcomes, including depression and suicide.

⇨ The above information is an extract from the Home Office document *Teenage Relationship Abuse: A Teacher's Guide to Violence and Abuse in Teenage Relationships*, and is reprinted with permission. Visit www.homeoffice.gov.uk for more information.

© Crown copyright

HOME OFFICE

Plight of teens abused by violent lovers

The scale of teenage domestic abuse was revealed today in a landmark study showing that children as young as 13 are suffering at the hands of violent partners.

By Kiran Randhawa, Health and Social Affairs Correspondent

Many victims are experiencing severe abuse such as being punched in the face or thrown down stairs.

More than half of girls and a quarter of boys questioned in the study, which focused on disadvantaged children, had been in a violent relationship before the age of 18.

A quarter of the girls said they had suffered severe violence such as being head-butted, slapped, punched or having earrings ripped out.

The teenagers, who were no longer in school for reasons including pregnancy, were almost twice as likely to suffer physical violence as girls in mainstream education.

When singer Rihanna spoke out after suffering violence at the hands of her boyfriend, rapper Chris Brown, in 2009, it was hoped other young victims would come forward.

> **A quarter of the girls said they had suffered severe violence such as being head-butted, slapped, punched or having earrings ripped out**

But most girls questioned by researchers from the NSPCC and Bristol University saw violence in relationships as normal.

Many victims said they were first attacked in their pre-teen years. A quarter of those surveyed revealed they had witnessed domestic violence in their family homes.

Two-thirds of girls and a third of boys said they had suffered emotional violence, such as being with a controlling partner.

Around half of girls thought this type of behaviour was normal. The Home Office is launching a campaign to challenge the attitudes of teenagers to violence and abuse in relationships but MPs and charity workers said more needs to be done.

Lisa Harker, head of strategy and development at the NSPCC, said: 'This research shows domestic violence is very much a teenage problem. Social workers, those working in the youth justice system and professionals who work with teenagers who have had to leave school, all need to be made aware of this.'

Home Office Minister Lynne Featherstone said: 'We need to challenge the attitudes that foster an acceptance of abusive relationships by intervening as early as possible. Bringing the issue out in the open will help teenagers feel confident to challenge abusive behaviour.'

'Older boyfriend forced me into sex'

Leonie Hodge was 13 when she suffered sexual abuse at the hands of her boyfriend.

Determined to be popular, she made friends with 'the wrong crowd' at school and through friends she met an 18-year-old who she began dating.

Weeks into the relationship, she was forced to perform a sexual act on him with his friends watching.

Miss Hodge, now 27, said: 'I was quite shy when I went to secondary school so I started hanging around with the popular crowd of girls who would meet up with boys a lot older.

'I soon began seeing an 18-year-old, which I thought was completely normal. He would ring me and I would lie to my family and go out and meet him in his friend's car.'

One night, she was picked up by his two friends and him. His friend parked up and despite her protests she was forced to carry out a sex act.

'I said I didn't want to and to let me out but they locked me in and forced me to,' she added.

'I was still a virgin and had never done anything like that. Afterwards I was in complete shock and was absolutely devastated.'

Miss Hodge, from Harrow, has set up a charity called Teen Boundaries to help educate young people on relationships and sexual bullying. For more information go to www.teenboundaries.co.uk.

⇨ This article first appeared in the *Evening Standard*, 14 September 2011

Where are the refuges for teenagers in abused relationships?

A study reveals that children as young as 13 are being physically, emotionally and sexually abused in their relationships. We must do more to help them escape.

By Carlene Firmin

A study funded by the NSPCC into teenage domestic abuse shows that over 50% of disadvantaged young women have been in violent relationships before their 18th birthday and children as young as 13 are being physically, emotionally and sexually abused in their relationships. Yet we still don't know how many young people are victimised each day but don't tell a soul. Assaulted in the shadows, the 'private' violence they experience influences their relationships with family, their choices, their health – and many agencies struggle to know how to respond.

Domestic violence is defined as taking place in a relationship between two adults. The historical legacy of this has seen the development of refuges, independent domestic violence advocates and risk assessment structures designed to keep women safe; creating conditions for them to leave relationships safely and regain control of their lives. This progress for women has been essential and rightly continues to seek investment and improvement to save and improve lives.

Professionals may be more aware that gender-based violence affects teenage as well as adult relationships, but support for specialist responses have not followed this awareness

But what of the violence that takes place in teenage relationships? We are yet to create conditions for girls to regain control and leave violent relationships safely. Women need to leave homes; girls' relationships take place in their schools, in their peer groups, in their neighbourhoods: how do they 'leave' these behind?

Professionals may be more aware that gender-based violence affects teenage as well as adult relationships, but support for specialist responses have not followed this awareness, constraining the choices that girls make and leaving them without the protection they desperately need.

Over the past three years, awareness that gang-related violence affects girls has increased dramatically. When I first started interviewing girls associated with gangs, the policy landscape was practically void of references to females, and lacked acknowledgement that girls may be in danger. Fast forward to 2011, and gang injunction guidance contains a specific chapter on young women, and references are made to gang-affected young women in plans to tackle violence against women.

One 18-year-old girl said to me: 'My boyfriend broke my nose when I was 15 and no one helped, no one has ever helped.'

Yet when girls are seeking to exit gang association or relationships with gang members, we haven't yet devised a gendered strategy to safely remove girls from such high-risk situations.

When a woman chooses to leave a violent relationship, her decision is influenced by many things, including the belief that refuges provide a safe haven. Without this safety net, how many would choose to leave? When people are the victims of crime they come forward to the police to be protected, to protect others and to seek justice; if they didn't believe this would be the outcome, would they choose to report?

One 18-year-old girl said to me: 'My boyfriend broke my nose when I was 15 and no one helped, no one has ever helped.' How distressing it must be to be aware of the risks you face yet believe that there is no help for you.

From prevention through to exit, children have a right to be protected from violence; the more we learn about the abuses against them, the more those who work with them need to ensure our responses can keep them safe.

Carlene Firmin is a principal policy adviser at the Office of the Children's Commissioner for England. She is writing in a personal capacity.

11 October 2011

THE GUARDIAN

Digital abuse in teen relationships

Information from loveisrespect.org.

Digital dating abuse is the use of technologies such as texting and social networking to bully, harass, stalk or intimidate a partner. Often this behaviour is a form of verbal or emotional abuse perpetrated online.

In a healthy relationship, all communication is respectful, whether in person, online or by phone. It is never OK for someone to do or say anything that makes you feel bad, lowers your self-esteem or manipulates you. You may be experiencing digital abuse if your partner:

⇨ tells you who you can or can't be friends with on Facebook and other sites;

⇨ sends you negative, insulting or even threatening emails, Facebook messages, tweets, DMs or other messages online;

⇨ uses sites like Facebook, Twitter and others to keep constant tabs on you;

⇨ puts you down in their status updates;

⇨ sends you unwanted, explicit pictures and demands you send some in return;

⇨ pressures you to send explicit video;

⇨ steals or insists to be given your passwords;

⇨ constantly texts you and makes you feel like you can't be separated from your phone for fear that you will be punished;

⇨ looks through your phone frequently, checks up on your pictures, texts and outgoing calls.

In a healthy relationship, all communication is respectful, whether in person, online or by phone

You never deserve to be mistreated, online or off. If you're experiencing digital dating abuse, we encourage you to chat with a peer advocate. Remember:

⇨ Your partner should respect your relationship boundaries.

⇨ It is OK to turn off your phone. You have the right to be alone and spend time with friends and family without your partner getting angry.

⇨ You do not have to text any pictures or statements that you are uncomfortable sending, especially nude or partially nude photos, known as 'sexting'.

⇨ You lose control of any electronic message once your partner receives it. They may forward it, so don't send anything you fear could be seen by others.

⇨ You do not have to share your passwords with anyone.

⇨ Know your privacy settings. Social networks such as Facebook allow the user to control how their information is shared and who has access to it. These are often customisable and are found in the privacy section of the site. Remember, registering for some applications (apps) requires you to change your privacy settings.

⇨ Be mindful when using check-ins like Facebook Places. Letting an abusive partner know where you are could be dangerous. Also, always ask your friends if it's OK for you to check them in. You never know if they are trying to keep their location secret.

⇨ Information from loveisrespect.org.

© loveisrespect.org

Sophie's story

Sophie, 17, has left her abusive boyfriend but he continues to harass her...

'm 17 and I was with my ex-boyfriend for six months. Before that I'd known him for a year and he was my best friend.

... he read all my text messages

Three months into the relationship everything changed. He became possessive and controlling. I wasn't allowed to see my friends and he didn't like me seeing family. If my phone rang he would answer it, and he read all my messages to check I was talking to no one else.

... at college I had to see him at every break

When I started college, he went there too and was in the year above me. After two months I couldn't face going

GETTING ON WITH THE REST OF MY —

there because he made me see him at every break. He would wait outside my lessons and even sometimes come into my lessons to have a go at me. Then it started with just the odd grab to stop me from going anywhere. Even when I was out with him he would hold onto me really tight so I couldn't move from his side.

... he badly sprained my wrist

One day at college he took my phone off me and told me to meet him after my lesson. He kept my phone so that I couldn't call anyone to pick me up. We got all the way to the station near my house where I had to get a bus, but then he wouldn't let me on the bus and held me against some metal gates while I cried, and then he dragged me off down the road. He badly sprained my wrist and I had to have a sling for a few days. I was utterly shocked that so many people could see what was happening, but just ignored it and didn't try to help. Even one of my old teachers from school walked past and ignored my crying.

... he slit his wrists in front of me

People tell you to 'just end it', but it's not that easy, as it can be the most dangerous time. When I ended the relationship, he slit his wrists in front of me with a knife, held me up against a wall and screamed abuse in my face. He would walk out into main roads and stand there waiting to be hit by a car. He even pushed me onto a main road, but luckily I got out of the way in time. Now every time I see him I shake and my heart comes up in my throat.

... I felt dependent on him

I managed to lose a lot of weight before I went out with him and he knew how happy it made me feel, but then he force-fed me so I would put on weight again because he said he didn't want other boys looking at me. He would bombard me with texts and phone calls. I once had over 200 hundred missed calls in three hours because I wouldn't answer my phone. But I would always go back to him because he told me he wouldn't do it again and he made me feel like I had no one but him. I felt dependent on him. I have so much respect for people who have left abusive relationships and I hope that one day I can fully get away from it myself.

⇨ The above information is reprinted from The Hideout with kind permission from Women's Aid Federation of England. Please visit their website at www.thehideout. org.uk for more information.

© Women's Aid

WOMEN's AID

When family life hurts: family experience of aggression in children

An update to Family Lives' October 2010 report.

In October 2010, Family Lives published a report exploring an issue that has been a growing trend on our helpline over the past few years: family experience of aggression in children. This report seeks once again to highlight this under-reported issue, adding new statistics

Every year, Parentline, Family Lives' free, round-the-clock family and parenting support telephone line, receives thousands of calls from distraught parents seeking help to manage their child's violent or aggressive behaviour. Last year's report analysed 83,469 long calls (classified as calls of a duration of 20 minutes or over) between the months of June 2008 and June 2010. This update looks at the 39,258 calls received by Parentline between July 2010 and June 2011.

> 'My son, Harry, had a temper tantrum last night over not doing his homework. I restrained him, as he was attempting to smash up his bedroom. My other children were terrified, my husband doesn't know what to do. Harry ripped my jeans and I have a huge bruise on my leg, he has smashed a hole in his door and ripped his light fitting out. We are all going to have to suffer this week because we have to pay to fix the damage. Harry just thinks it's all unfair on him! We are in a dark place right now, I know I need help with this, but am terrified of the consequences for Harry.'
>
> *Mother of teenage son*

Incidences of physical or verbal aggression are a part of normal child development, and dealing with them presents important learning and growth opportunities for both parent and child. However, our data suggests that a steadily increasing minority of families are battling with more entrenched and complex problems that point towards concerns around their child's emotional and mental health. It is the growing minority that form the focus of this report.

Data from Parentline shows that families calling about aggression in children are more likely to report that their children are not enjoying good mental health and wellbeing. Many appear to be displaying behaviours associated with conduct disorders and a number of families are already in contact with specialist Child and Adolescent Mental Health Services (CAMHS). Conduct disorders are the most common childhood psychiatric disorders.[1]

At a family level, interventions that are known to reduce levels of violence and abuse include parental mental health promotion, parent training and early intervention for child emotional and behavioural disorders.[2] Yet Family Lives' experience is that all too often, by the time many families seek help they are in a desperate position and some require intensive interventions, such as children being taken away by the police or social services. The stigma attached to the abuse can prevent families from seeking help early and preventing the problem form spiralling out of control.

> **Data from Parentline shows that families calling about aggression in children are more likely to report that their children are not enjoying good mental health and wellbeing**

A large number of calls to Parentline – Family Lives' free, national helpline – have consistently concerned children's behaviour. This section highlights the trends and points of difference in our data between the last report, which looked at calls between June 2008 and June 2010, and a new set of data looking at calls from July 2010 to June 2011.

The most striking finding from the data is that calls about aggression have continued to rise: in this report calls about a child's physical aggression have risen by 2% and calls about a child's verbal aggression have risen by 4%.

Much of the data in this report was consistent with the last report.

Aggression in the home

The vast majority of callers were concerned about aggression in the home, rather than in school or another setting. This had risen by 1% to 89% of those calling about their child's aggressive behaviour.

FAMILY LIVES

Mothers

Mothers bear the brunt of their child's aggressive behaviour, although in many cases this does spill out to others in the family. 72% of all long calls were from mothers, yet 80.5% of calls about children's behaviour were from mothers.

Girls and boys

Contrary to public perception, this is an issue that crosses the gender divide. Boys and girls are physically and verbally aggressive in similar numbers, although boys are slightly more likely to be both physically and verbally aggressive.

Early teens

Aggressive behaviour is reported in children of all ages, but peaks in children aged between 13 and 15 years old. In calls to Parentline, 42.9% of calls about behaviour related to children aged 13–15 years, compared to 26% of all long calls relating to that age group.[3]

Where aggression was the main feature of the call to Parentline, children were more likely to have emotional problems, poor wellbeing and/or mental health problems

---

Verbal aggression has marginally increased since June 2009–June 2010 for children up to nine years of age. Physical aggression has increased by 4.5% since June 2009–June 2010 for 10- to 15-year-olds.

Experience of parents

Parents and carers facing aggressive behaviour from their children report feeling desperate, helpless, ashamed and out of control. Parents calling about their child's aggression were 30.3% more likely to suffer from stress than other callers, and 8.3% more likely to be suffering with anger.

Children's mental health

Where aggression was the main feature of the call to Parentline, children were more likely to have emotional problems, poor wellbeing and/or mental health problems. Children are more likely to suffer from identified (2.1%) or unidentified (4.9%) depression if they have behavioural issues compared to all long calls (1.2% and 2.5%, respectively). Self-harm is more likely to be reported (2.6% compared to 1.3%), as is suicide (2.4% compared

to 1.2%), hyperactivity (3.3% compared to 1.3%) and isolation (5.1% compared to 3.2%).

Compared to June 2009–June 2010 statistics, stress, confusion, isolation and anger have increased by an average of 5.3% where a child is being verbally aggressive and by 5.4% in calls where a child is physically aggressive.

Crime

Aggressive behaviour was also linked to higher incidences of involvement with the youth justice system, gang involvement and weapon-carrying, smoking, anti-social behaviour and children wanting to leave home. Children who were verbally aggressive were more likely to be involved with the youth justice system (3.6% of calls compared to 0.9% of all calls) and significantly more likely to have issues with lying (18.4% compared to 4.5% of all calls). Children who are physically aggressive were significantly more likely to be using drugs (10.1% compared to 3.2% of all calls) and to be in with a bad crowd (10.9% compared to 3.4% of all calls).

References

1   Green H, McGinnity A, Meltzer H, et al (2005) *Mental Health of Children and Young People in Great Britain, 2004*. Office for National Statistics.

2   Royal College of Psychiatrists (2010) *No health without public mental health: the case for action, Position statement*, PS4/2010.

3   In our web survey, the majority of respondents (24%) were concerned about aggression in 10- to 12-year-olds.

June 2011

⇨ The above information is an extract from Family Lives' report *When Family Life Hurts: Family Experience of Aggression in Children*, an update to Family Lives' October 2010 report. Visit www.familylives.org.uk for more.

Effects of domestic abuse on children and young people

Information from Welsh Women's Aid.

Prevalence

The Department of Health estimates that every year, 750,000 children experience domestic abuse. However, as many cases of domestic abuse go unreported, the actual figures are likely to be higher than this. In addition to this, it is estimated that women will experience on average 35 incidents of domestic abuse before contacting the police. As a result of this, it is very likely that in homes where children are present, their experiences of domestic abuse also go unreported, thus leaving these children living with the impacts of abuse.

The Department of Health estimates that every year, 750,000 children experience domestic abuse

Section 120 of the Adoption and Children Act 2002 extended the definition of what constitutes 'significant harm' to children to include:

'Any impairment of the child's health or development as a result of witnessing the ill treatment of another person such as domestic violence.'

The Act makes clear that ill treatment is broader than physical violence and includes forms of ill treatment that are not physical, such as seeing a person being harassed or intimidated by another person.

Experiences

Children and young people's experiences of domestic abuse can vary depending on the situation, type and extent of domestic abuse occurring within the home. They may:

⇨ witness the abuse – including physical and sexual violence, other abusive behaviours, hearing arguments, and seeing the physical and emotional effects of abuse;

⇨ intervene to try and stop the abuse – in order to protect their mum or other family members;

⇨ be directly abused themselves;

⇨ be forced to join in with abusive acts by the abuser;

⇨ experience domestic abuse/unhealthy relationships within their own interpersonal relationships in their teenage years.

It is important to note that all children and young people may experience domestic abuse and be affected by it in different ways. The extent of the impact of domestic abuse can depend on factors such as: severity, frequency, type of abuse, length of time witnessing abuse, age, stage of development and family dynamics. Even children from the same family, subjected to the same type of domestic abuse, may experience it and be affected by it differently.

Indicators

The list below offers possible indicators that may be a sign that a child or young person is experiencing domestic abuse:

⇨ A direct disclosure is made by the child/young person.

⇨ Injuries.

⇨ Poor school attendance/achievement.

⇨ Low self-esteem and confidence.

⇨ Anxiety.

⇨ Lack of concentration.

⇨ Withdrawal.

⇨ Behavioural problems.

In almost one-third (30%) of cases, domestic abuse begins or escalates during pregnancy

Effects

The range of potential effects of domestic abuse on children and young people is vast, ranging from lack of sleep through to the loss of life. The effects can be divided into age categories as outlined below:

Unborn babies

In almost one-third (30%) of cases, domestic abuse begins or escalates during pregnancy. As a result, there is a link between miscarriages, premature birth and the medical problems that are linked to this.

Infants

⇨ Irritability.

⇨ Poor sleep patterns.

⇨ Clinginess.

⇨ Tantrums.

⇨ Delayed development – e.g. speech and walking.

Pre-school children

⇨ Physical complaints – e.g. a bad tummy/head.

⇨ Bedwetting.

⇨ Baby-like behaviours.

⇨ Withdrawal.

⇨ Sleeping problems – nightmares, reluctance to go to bed.

⇨ Tendency to 'whine'.

⇨ Fear of certain people.

⇨ Aggression.

Primary school-age children

⇨ Continued physical complaints.

⇨ Withdrawal/isolation/poor social skills – no friendship groups.

⇨ Excessive approval seeking – e.g. 'mum's helper'/ 'teacher's pet'.

⇨ Aggression and temper tantrums.

⇨ Bullying/being bullied.

⇨ Eating disorders.

⇨ Sleeping problems.

⇨ Regressive behaviours.

Secondary school-age children/adolescents

⇨ Substance misuse.

⇨ Running away from home.

⇨ Self-harm.

⇨ Violent thoughts/behaviours.

⇨ Eating disorders.

⇨ Low self-esteem.

⇨ Difficulty in establishing their own healthy relationships – at risk of experiencing dating abuse.

Please note, the above lists are meant as a guideline only of SOME of the possible effects of domestic abuse, and this list is not exhaustive.

Roles taken on by children and young people

Many children and young people who are experiencing domestic abuse often take on certain 'roles' within the family. This may happen unconsciously for the child, or they may have the roles forced upon them. The roles that children adopt can also be linked to how they interpret and learn to cope with the domestic abuse they live with. Examples of roles include:

⇨ Caretaker.

⇨ Mother's confidante.

⇨ Perfect child.

⇨ Referee.

⇨ Scapegoat.

⇨ Abuser's confidante.

⇨ Abuser's helper.

⇨ The above information is reproduced with kind permission from Welsh Women's Aid. Visit www. welshwomensaid.org for more information on this and other related topics.

Sam's story

Information from Refuge.

Refuge
For women and children.
Against domestic violence.

Sam, aged three and a half years, arrived at Refuge with his mum and three sisters. His mum met with the pre-school psychologist soon after their arrival and discussed her concerns about Sam and his fear of going to the toilet. Through talking with the psychologist it emerged that Sam also had difficulties sleeping and was very quiet and withdrawn. He had regressed to younger behaviours of wearing a nappy and wanting a bottle: he also displayed many symptoms of post-traumatic stress, including being very jumpy and having nightmares about violence.

When the family lived at home much of the violence occurred late at night. Sam would often get out of bed and stand at the top of the stairs to listen and see what was happening. He saw his father screaming, shouting, throwing objects, breaking furniture, as well as hitting his mother. Sam would stand there, frozen and shaking with fear, or sometimes crying and screaming. Not surprisingly, he continued to have sleep problems and would wake several times in the night, becoming extremely distressed if his mother was not there beside him.

The Refuge team used play as a way to understand Sam's experiences. During play with the dolls' house, Sam at first refused to include his dad in the set of dolls which represented his family members. When he eventually allowed the psychologist to introduce a 'dad doll' into the play, Sam threw the doll away, took the car and ran over the doll, saying 'run him over'. Later, his older sister asked Sam why he threw his dad

away and Sam replied: 'I didn't want him in the house.' For the first time Sam's experiences and feelings were acknowledged as being real and he had an opportunity to take control of a situation which he was once powerless to do anything about.

In further sessions Sam became more able to verbally express what he had seen, telling the psychologist that 'daddy hit mummy' and it was 'very sad'. He learnt more about feelings through using pictures of faces and talked about 'daddy's angry face', 'mummy's sad face' and his own 'scared face'.

After just three sessions Sam's mother could not believe how much Sam had changed. She reported that for the first time when Sam had woken and she was not there, Sam had not screamed, but had calmly got up to see where she was. He had become able to do things for himself rather than remaining stuck, distressed and traumatised. He became less clingy with his mum and was much more confident and talkative around other people, even making jokes. The family was re-housed shortly after this and his mum continues to help Sam feel safe and secure.

⇨ Information from Refuge. Visit www.refuge.org.uk for more information.

© Refuge

Teenage rape prevention

Information from the Home Office.

The teenage rape prevention campaign, launched on 5 March 2012, aims to prevent teenagers from becoming victims and perpetrators of sexual violence and abuse.

As part of the Violence Against Women and Girls Action Plan, the campaign encourages teenagers to rethink their views on rape, sexual assault, violence and abuse, and direct them to places for help and advice.

Building on the success of the campaign against teenage relationship abuse, this campaign targets 13- to 18-year-old boys and girls to specifically focus on rape and sexual assault. The campaign aims to:

⇨ raise awareness of the issue of rape and sexual violence;

⇨ improve understanding of what constitutes rape, sexual assault and consent;

⇨ empower young people to avoid, challenge and report sexually violent behaviour.

The campaign website www.thisisabuse.direct.gov.uk gives teenagers the change to discuss the issues with their peers and get access to third-party support and advice.

⇨ Information from the Home Office. Visit www.homeoffice.gov.uk for more information.

© Crown copyright 2012

Domestic violence costs £5.5 billion a year

New analysis, released today by Trust for London and the Henry Smith Charity, highlights the costs of domestic violence to the public purse across England – a minimum of £5 million each week in every region.

The release of these figures coincides with the launch of a new report, *Islands in the Stream*, which demonstrates the effectiveness and low cost of specialist support for high-risk victims and makes recommendations on how to improve domestic violence services across the country.

In England the estimated total costs of domestic violence are £5.5 billion, which comprises:

 £1.6bn for physical & mental health costs

 £1.2bn in criminal justice costs

 £268m in social services costs

 £185.7m in housing and refuge costs

 £366.7m in civil legal costs

 £1.8bn in lost economic output

The highest total costs in England are in the following areas:

⇨ London (£918 million)

⇨ South East (£872.6 million)

⇨ North West (£720 million)

⇨ East of England (£590.5 million).

In addition, the human and emotional costs in England are estimated to be almost £26 million per day.

Commenting on the figures, Davina James-Hanman, domestic violence advisor to Trust for London and Henry Smith Charity, said:

'These figures reveal the huge financial impact domestic violence has across every region and the stress it puts on everything from housing and the NHS to social services. In a climate of cuts, a reduction in specialist domestic violence services would be a false economy.

'Our forthcoming report calculates that an independent domestic violence advocate supporting a client at high risk costs on average £500. The estimated cost of a domestic violence homicide is approximately £1 million, so the economic as well as the moral argument is compelling.

> *The human and emotional costs [of domestic violence] in England are estimated to be almost £26 million per day*

'We are therefore calling on local and central government to ensure that services are well co-ordinated locally and provide comprehensive support to victims at low, medium and high risk to respond to the devastating, and potentially fatal, effects of domestic violence.'

27 January 2011

⇨ The above information is reproduced with kind permission from Trust for London. Please visit www.trustforlondon.org.uk for more information on this and other related topics.

© 2011 Trust for London

TRUST FOR LONDON

A different world is possible

A call for long-term and targeted action to prevent violence against women and girls. Report summary 2011.

Call to action: a different world is possible!

Violence against women has been described as 'perhaps the most pervasive violation of human rights across the globe'. This violence bears significant costs – for individuals, for public services, society and the economy. Violence against women and girls (VAWG) is more prevalent amongst women in England than stroke, diabetes and heart disease. Yet the prevention of VAWG has been a long-neglected part of Westminster government policy.

> The End Violence Against Women coalition (EVAW) is calling for a coordinated, targeted and long-term approach to preventing violence against women and girls (VAWG). In particular, we are calling for schools and other educational institutions to play their part in creating a safer world for women and girls. At an estimated cost of around £122,000 per rape and a total annual health cost for domestic violence at around £1,100,000,000, the benefits of preventing violence in the first place will far outweigh the costs.

What is this report?

The *A different world is possible* report sets out why we need a targeted and long-term approach to preventing VAWG drawing on the most cutting-edge evidence base on the causal factors underlying violence and abuse. We make policy recommendations under ten areas of action for Westminster government departments, statutory bodies, schools and other educational institutions and local authorities, providing a preliminary blueprint for decision-makers and an advocacy tool for the third sector. The report has been developed with expert practitioners, researchers and policy analysts on the EVAW Prevention Network, England. The report is complemented with *A Different World is Possible: Promising practices to prevent violence against women and girls*, a piece of research that explores innovative examples of interventions to prevent violence through education, community mobilisation and capacity-building, media and public awareness. The intended audience for the report is Members of Parliament, civil servants, local authorities, schools, policy-makers, violence against women and girls organisations and other organisations who are interested in ending VAWG.

Why do we need a targeted and long-term approach to prevention?

Violence against women and girls is widespread, as are attitudes that normalise and excuse this violence.

⇨ Up to three million women across the UK experience rape, domestic violence, forced marriage, stalking, sexual exploitation and trafficking, female genital mutilation (FGM) or so-called honour violence each year.

⇨ Almost one in three girls have experienced unwanted sexual touching at school.

⇨ Over one in three people believe that a woman should be held wholly or partly responsible for being sexually assaulted or raped if she was drunk.

Up to three million women across the UK experience rape, domestic violence, forced marriage, stalking, sexual exploitation and trafficking, female genital mutilation (FGM) or so-called honour violence each year

⇨ 33 per cent of girls in an intimate relationship aged 13 to 17 have experienced some form of sexual violence from a partner.

⇨ In 2009 the Forced Marriage Unit received over 1,600 calls to its helpline on suspected/potential forced marriage, 86 per cent of which were from women.

> 'You have to show how masculine you are; you can't show sensitivity – it is difficult to be different – you need to look and act a certain way.' *Young man, Year 11*

Violence against women has serious consequences for individuals and society.

⇨ Women and girls who experience violence endure significant physical, emotional, health, financial and social consequences. Violence causes physical

damage ranging from death in extreme cases to miscarriages, broken limbs and cuts and bruises.

⇨ It is estimated that violence against women costs society £40 billion each year in England and Wales.

Governments have obligations to prevent violence against women under international and national human rights and equality laws.

⇨ Under the European Convention on Human Rights and the Convention on the Elimination of All Forms of Discrimination Against Women (CEDAW), the UK has obligations to exercise due diligence in preventing violence against women before it happens.

⇨ In Britain, the Public Sector Equality Duty under the Equality Act 2010 requires public bodies to take account of how they are promoting equality between women and men. Under the new duty, public bodies should be considering how they are preventing VAWG.

> 'I have started wearing shorts underneath my skirt as boys lift up skirts as they walk by...sometimes they come up behind you and put their hands on your chest.' *Young woman, Year 9*

The current policy context

Current Westminster VAWG policy makes prevention a priority – a commitment which is long overdue and welcome. However, although the Coalition Government's *Call to End Violence Against Women and Girls: Action Plan* contains some positive developments, it lacks: an investment in research, monitoring or evaluation; a concerted effort to embed prevention work in educational settings; a commitment to long-term and evidence-based public awareness campaigns; and adequate and sustained funding of the VAWG sector to deliver their services and prevention programmes. The current ad hoc approach to prevention is short-sighted, costly and unlikely to deliver the change needed to truly eliminate VAWG.

Schools must play their part in ending violence against women and girls

Educational settings are an important site of prevention where attitudes that condone VAWG and gender stereotypes can be challenged and positive attitudes towards gender equality and equal relationships can be fostered. There are significant long-term social and economic gains to be made by investing in prevention through education. However, schools and academies – key players in delivering prevention – are on the back foot in responding to violence against women and girls

with a weak response. This means they may not be meeting their legal obligations under child protection and equality law to provide safe environments and teach students about healthy, respectful and equal relationships. In this report, we call for all primary and secondary schools, including academies, to play their part in ending VAWG.

All primary and secondary schools, including academies, should:

⇨ develop and implement a 'whole-school approach' to prevent VAWG;

⇨ appoint VAWG champions amongst school governors and student councils;

⇨ directly commission VAWG services to design and deliver targeted prevention interventions;

⇨ ensure access for students to specialist VAWG support services in the community; and

⇨ ensure that their anti-bullying policies include an explicit reference to sexual harassment and bullying.

All local authorities should:

⇨ establish local partnerships with relevant voluntary sector agencies, primary and secondary schools to support the co-ordinated delivery of prevention work; and

⇨ champion a 'whole-school approach' to preventing VAWG amongst primary and secondary schools, including academies, in their area.

The Greater London Authority should:

⇨ champion a 'whole-school approach' to preventing VAWG amongst primary and secondary schools, including academies, in the Greater London area; and

⇨ regularly communicate through public messages the important role of educational institutions in preventing VAWG.

> 'Schools are a microcosm of society in general. You have a chance when you are dealing with young people to change attitudes ... I think if you don't take a stand over it you are basically colluding.' *School teacher*

The Minister for Education and Department for Education should:

⇨ amend the Education Bill 2011 to make it a requirement for all schools and academies to collect and report data on all forms of violence against young women and girls in schools, including sexual harassment and bullying;

- ⇨ communicate to all primary and secondary schools, including academies, the importance of addressing VAWG through a whole-school approach;

- ⇨ appoint a senior policy lead who is responsible for developing and implementing a department-wide action plan on VAWG;

- ⇨ work with organisations like the Centre for Excellence and Outcomes to ensure examples of best practice are disseminated widely across primary and secondary schools, including academies;

- ⇨ ensure initial and ongoing training for teaching and non-teaching school staff and governors to increase awareness and build skills to challenge VAWG;

Ten areas of action to prevent violence against women and girls

The prevention of VAWG requires a range of targeted interventions which are designed and delivered in a co-ordinated manner:

1 Develop and implement a cross-government gender equality strategy.

2 Ensure universal delivery of a 'whole-school approach' to prevent violence against women and girls across the education system.

3 Ensure funding for specialist violence against women and girls services to deliver prevention work.

4 Invest in research, monitoring and evaluation of prevention interventions.

5 Produce evidence-based and sustained public awareness campaigns.

6 Fund community mobilisation activities to challenge violence against women and girls.

7 Promote leadership at all levels to champion gender equality and non-violent norms.

8 Tackle the sexualisation of women and girls in the media and popular culture.

9 Commission the voluntary VAWG sector to deliver quality training on violence against women and girls to a range of agencies as part of vocational qualifications and ongoing professional development.

10 Target interventions to ensure prevention of violence against women and girls addresses intersections of gender with other social inequalities.

- ⇨ under the Public Sector Equality Duty, set an objective on tackling VAWG in primary and secondary schools – they should regularly collect, analyse and publish data on young women's and girls' experiences of all forms of violence and require regular school surveys on experiences of violence and attitudes;

- ⇨ develop specific strategies to ensure the safety and wellbeing of girls in Pupil Referral Units and consider alternative behaviour management strategies for girls;

33 per cent of girls in an intimate relationship aged 13 to 17 have experienced some form of sexual violence from a partner

- ⇨ integrate gender stereotypes, sexualisation, VAWG and media literacy into the primary and secondary curriculum across all subjects in an age-appropriate manner as part of the National Curriculum review;

- ⇨ make Sex and Relationship Education (SRE) and Personal, Social, Health and Economic education (PSHE) part of the statutory curriculum to ensure universal access for all students; and

- ⇨ ensure the internal review of PSHE and SRE addresses VAWG. References on sexualisation, VAWG, healthy relationships, gender stereotypes,

media literacy and the harms of pornography should be included in the Department's guidance on Sex and Relationship Education.

Ofsted should:

⇨ ensure inspection judgements on behaviour and safety assess how well schools are tackling VAWG including sexual harassment and bullying, looking for evidence of all forms of violence against girls in schools; and

⇨ carry out a thematic review/survey into how well primary and secondary schools are tackling VAWG.

The Education Select Committee should:

⇨ conduct an inquiry into how schools are responding to VAWG.

The Equality and Human Rights Commission should:

⇨ support schools, academies and colleges to meet their obligations to prevent violence against young women and girls under the Public Sector Equality Duty by producing specific guidance; and

⇨ regularly monitor schools, academies and colleges to ensure compliance with the Public Sector Equality Duty and take action where necessary.

Take action to create a different world for women and girls

Based on the recommendations of this report, EVAW is campaigning for greater action from the Department for Education, local authorities and schools on preventing VAWG through education. Visit www.endviolenceagainstwomen.org.uk to download our campaign actions and template letters.

About the End Violence Against Women Coalition

The End Violence Against Women (EVAW) Coalition campaigns for governments at all levels around the UK to take urgent action to eliminate all forms of violence against women and girls. We are the largest coalition of its kind in the UK, representing over seven million individuals and organisations. A full list of members is on our website.

June 2011

⇨ The above information is an extract from the EVAW's report *A Different World is Possible*, and is reprinted with permission. Visit www.endviolenceagainstwomen.org.uk for more information.

© *The End Violence Against Women Coalition*

Make My Day

Song written and recorded by a young person attending Morgan Academy, Dundee. Played at the 'Our Rights' event.

It all begun when I saw my dad hit my mum

Through a key hole I'd look

To see my mum's life being took, you see

Sometime I'd have to run

He'd take his belt off and say you're next son

Can't quite describe the fear

Whenever that man is near

Sometimes he'd say go to your room

Get half way through then

Boom, boom, boom then smack, smack,

Boom

The best would crack her near the eye

It's this man, I pure despise

The neighbours say they can hear her cries

Tear drops dripping from her eyes

Me on my own I sit in silence

Whenever I'm away from the violence

Think of a place by myself, with nobody else

In school it travels the news,

About me and how I've got a new bruise

On my cheek a little to the left

I'm actually considering death

Cause suicide, seems like the only way

To make my day

To make my dad pay

No-one listens to what I say.....!

UK must send a clear message on domestic violence

A new Council of Europe treaty will make a real difference to abuse sufferers – so why is our government so reluctant to sign?

By Gauri van Gulik

Ministers from countries all across Europe gathered in Istanbul today to sign a new Council of Europe convention on domestic violence at the Istanbul summit of the committee of ministers. Incredibly, the UK wasn't one of the signatories. The British Government so far has not commented on its reasoning, but for a country that prides itself on being a leader on women's rights, its failure to sign so far is both a mystery and a serious disappointment.

The UK Government has been sending out mixed messages when it comes to domestic violence, as Jon Robins has pointed out before. On the one hand, the Home Secretary, Theresa May, and the Director of Public Prosecutions stress how serious this violence is and how determined they are to end it. On the other, the Government is nibbling away determinedly at those services that are needed to fight violence, such as legal aid and protection for female asylum seekers who suffered domestic violence in their home country.

The UK Government has been sending out mixed messages when it comes to domestic violence

And now it is reluctant to sign a groundbreaking new treaty that will truly make a difference throughout the European region.

The UK's leadership and support is important not just at home but for the whole region, as my research about domestic violence in Turkey shows.

Born in south-eastern Turkey, Selvi was 22 years old and pregnant with her fifth child when I met her while conducting research for a report on domestic violence. Her husband started his attacks when she was pregnant with their first child. 'That first time, he hit me, he kicked the baby in my belly, and he threw me off the roof,' she said. In 2008, Selvi (her name has been changed for her protection) finally went to the police after her husband had repeatedly raped her and broken her skull and arm. But the police, after questioning her husband at the station, told Selvi: 'There's no problem, we spoke

to him, you're back together.' This happened three more times. 'I just cannot go to the police any more,' she said.

Selvi's story encapsulates everything that can go horribly wrong when domestic violence is not taken seriously.

'That first time, he hit me, he kicked the baby in my belly, and he threw me off the roof'

The landmark new Council of Europe convention on preventing and combating violence against women and domestic violence offers a comprehensive international legal instrument to address this type of abuse, and includes a monitoring mechanism to ensure its provisions are implemented.

Implementation is crucial, for Selvi's case is sadly not isolated. Less than five miles from the site where the convention was being signed, Zelal (not her real name) lives with her three children across the street from her ex-husband's home. One day, he grabbed her as she walked out of her house. She explained: 'He held me, I screamed, "Let me go." He started beating me. There were a lot of people around us, but nobody did anything. He pulled my hair and covered my mouth, and he dragged me to my house. There he kicked me and I fell to the ground ... He broke every possession I have in the house, every chair, every picture, everything. Then he took off my clothes and he raped me.'

Zelal managed to escape, almost naked, and went to two different police stations, where she endured a barrage of questions, from, 'Aren't you ashamed to tell me you were raped by your ex-husband?' to 'Why are you bothering us with this?' She eventually managed to speak with a prosecutor, but he told her to come back after the weekend.

Zelal's ordeal is one of many documented in a new Human Rights Watch report on family violence in Turkey. The report documents the awful experiences of women of all ages in Istanbul, Ankara, Izmir, Van, Trabzon and Diyarbakir as they endured violence and sought help from the state. Women and girls as young as 14 told of being raped, stabbed, kicked in the stomach when

pregnant, beaten with hammers, sticks, branches and hoses to the point of broken bones and fractured skulls, locked up with dogs or other animals, starved, shot with a stun gun, injected with poison, pushed off a rooftop, and subjected to severe psychological violence.

In Turkey, 42% of all women have experienced such physical or sexual violence committed by a husband or partner, according to a major university study. Turkey has implemented important legislative changes to its penal and civil codes to deal with this crisis, including the establishment of a legal framework for the protection of domestic violence survivors, giving them the option of requesting a protection order.

In Turkey, 42% of all women have experienced physical or sexual violence committed by a husband or partner

However, there are serious shortcomings in the implementation of these reforms. The Turkish Government had helped a few women we interviewed, but many others said that police, prosecutors and judges sent them back to their abusers or acted so slowly on emergency protection orders that their very purpose was defeated. Too few domestic violence shelters offer protection, and some even keep their doors shut for victims lacking proper documentation, or women with disabilities.

The Turkish Government, which largely has good laws on the books, must systematically and actively improve their implementation and guarantee access to protection and justice for women like Selvi or Zelal who desperately need it.

How can we end this pandemic of violence against women and girls that still affects a quarter of all women in Europe?

The European signatories to the new convention gathered in Istanbul can learn from Turkey's experience. Strong legislation is necessary to fight domestic violence, but it is not enough. Every woman who survives violence should have access to protection, whatever her ethnic background, legal status, sexual orientation, marital status, economic situation or profession.

The UK should start by signing the Council of Europe convention, not just for women in the UK, but to send a clear message to all other countries in the region: take the struggle against violence seriously

The UK should start by signing the Council of Europe convention, not just for women in the UK, but to send a clear message to all other countries in the region: take the struggle against violence seriously.

19 May 2011

YOUR HUSBAND SAYS YOU'RE FREE TO GO HOME...

THE GUARDIAN

What constitutes domestic abuse?

Cross-government definition of domestic violence: a consultation.

Foreword from Theresa May, the Home Secretary

Everybody should feel safe within their own home. But for too many women in the UK, their home is actually one of the most dangerous places to be. On average two women are murdered by their current or former partner each week. Each year around 1.2 million women suffer domestic violence. Around one in four women will experience domestic abuse in their lifetime, often accompanied by years of psychological abuse. This just should not happen in modern day Britain. And that is why I am so determined to end domestic violence.

As we set out in our strategic vision – *Call to End Violence Against Women and Girls* – prevention will be key to achieving that ambition. Effective prevention can only happen when it involves all agencies, working together to common goals and a common understanding. That is why we are now consulting on the definition of domestic violence that all agencies and all parts of government should use.

Domestic violence ruins lives. Sadly, in some cases it ends them

There are a number of aspects to the definition that this consultation considers. The British Crime Survey has found that women between 16 and 24 years of age and men aged between 16 and 34 years of age were more likely to suffer relationship abuse than any other age range. That is why this consultation seeks views on whether the definition of domestic violence should include younger victims, including boys.

We also know that abuse may often include coercive control. Coercive control is a complex pattern of abuse using power and psychological control over another – financial control, verbal abuse, forced social isolation. These incidents may vary in seriousness and may be repeated over time. However, coercive control is not currently reflected in the Government's definition of domestic violence. We would welcome views on whether it should be.

Domestic violence ruins lives. Sadly, in some cases it ends them. This consultation will help us achieve the right agreed definition of domestic violence so that all agencies can work together to defeat this dreadful crime.

About the consultation

The Government seeks views on the desirability of revising the definition of domestic violence. There are four options for consideration.

Option 1 – the Government's definition of domestic violence remains the same

In 2004, the Government introduced a single definition of domestic violence, replacing the previous different definitions in use across government and the public sector. The definition is not a statutory definition. It is used by government departments to inform policy development and, for example, by police, the Crown Prosecution Service and the UK Border Agency, to inform the identification of domestic violence cases. The current definition defines domestic violence as:

'Any incident of threatening behaviour, violence or abuse [psychological, physical, sexual, financial or emotional] between adults who are or have been intimate partners or family members, regardless of gender or sexuality.'

This definition includes so-called 'honour'-based violence, female genital mutilation (FGM) and forced marriage, and is clear that victims are not confined to one gender or ethnic group. An adult is defined as any person aged 18 years or over.

We recognise that domestic violence may be perpetrated by family, extended family members and within communities and this can make it even more difficult for victims to speak out about the abuse.

We know that differing definitions can be problematic for victims as they may be recognised as such by some services and not by others.

Our aim is to ensure that we have a consistent definition of domestic violence. The Government seeks views on whether the current definition of domestic violence is working and should remain.

Option 2 – the definition of domestic violence is amended to include coercive control

The Government definition identifies domestic violence as 'incidents of threatening behaviour, violence or abuse.'

Other administrations have defined domestic violence in a broader way. The Welsh Government, for example, currently work to the following definition:

'Domestic abuse is best described as the use of physical and/or emotional abuse or violence, including undermining of self-confidence, sexual violence or the threat of violence,

HOME OFFICE

by a person who is or has been in a close relationship. 'Domestic abuse can go beyond actual physical violence. It can also involve emotional abuse, the destruction of a spouse's or partner's property, their isolation from friends, family or other potential sources of support, threats to others including children, control over access to money, personal items, food, transportation and the telephone, and stalking.

'It can also include violence perpetrated by a son, daughter or any other person who has a close or blood relationship with the victim/survivor. It can also include violence inflicted on, or witnessed by, children. The wide adverse effects of living with domestic abuse for children must be recognised as a child protection issue. The effects can be linked to poor educational achievement, social exclusion and to juvenile crime, substance abuse, mental health problems and homelessness from running away.

'Domestic abuse is not a "one-off" occurrence; it is frequent and persistent.'

Domestic violence is often underpinned by a pattern of coercive control. Coercive control is a complex pattern of overlapping and repeated abuse perpetrated within a context of power and control. It can be described as a series of repeated incidents which may vary from lesser to greater severity. This could include things like the control of finances, verbal abuse or isolation which may include control over whom a person can see or where they can go. Psychological control is a unique factor that sets domestic violence apart from other types of crime. Such control could also include a person being forced to change their behaviour as a result of fear.

Without the inclusion of coercive control in the definition of domestic violence, there may be occasions where domestic violence could be regarded as an isolated incident. As a result, it may be unclear to victims what counts as domestic violence – for example, it may be thought to include physical violence only. We know that the first incident reported to the police or other agencies is rarely the first incident to occur; often people have been subject to abuse on multiple occasions before they seek help.

Option 3 – the Government's definition of domestic violence is extended to 16- to 17-year-olds and Option 4 – the Government's definition of domestic violence is extended to all those under 18

In 2008, the Home Affairs Select Committee report *Domestic Violence, Forced Marriage and 'Honour' Based-Violence (HBV)* stated that:

'We heard of concerning attitudes and abuse between young people in intimate relationships. However, 16- to 18-year-olds are excluded from the current government definition of domestic violence, there has

been little research on the needs of teenage victims and perpetrators of domestic violence, and there is little support for under-18s in abusive relationships. The existence of abuse in teenage relationships further underlines the urgent need for effective early education on domestic violence and relationships.' (Paragraph 76)

We welcome the research being carried out by Respect and the NSPCC with the Big Lottery Fund. We recommend that the Government consider amending its definition of domestic violence to include under-18s. The full report can be found at: www.publications.parliament. uk/pa/cm200708/cmselect/cmhaff/263/263i.pdf

A commitment to consider this change was made in the *Violence Against Women and Girls Action Plan*, published in March 2011:

'Following a recommendation from the Home Affairs Select Committee report in 2008, the \government will consult on a revised definition of domestic violence to include victims under 18 years of age.'

We are concerned by the reported attitudes of some young people in relation to the acceptability of abuse. Currently, those under 18 years of age are excluded from the domestic violence definition. At present, domestic violence committed against a person under 18 would be considered child abuse by most services. Whilst this may be appropriate for children experiencing parental or family-based violence, there is the suggestion that the nature of teenage relationships is often more similar to relationships between adults and as such could be considered as an extension of adult domestic violence.

In the current cross-government definition we refer to 'intimate partner'; however, studies into the prevalence of teenage relationship abuse use different definitions for relationships that reflect the more fluid, less narrow labels used for describing relationships between and with under-18s. Non-cohabiting couples are more likely in teenage relationships than in adult relationships and a 'date' can take many different forms.

We have set out below some examples to demonstrate why this issue should be explored further.

Teenage relationship abuse

The 2009/10 British Crime Survey (BCS) found that young people were more likely to suffer partner abuse in the last year than any other age range. The 2009/10 BCS found 12.7% of women and 6.2% of men aged 16–19 had experienced some form of domestic abuse in the last year. Anecdotal evidence has also shown there are worryingly high levels of acceptance of abuse in teenage relationships.

It is important to consider that people can be married aged 16 in England and Wales, provided they have consent from their parents or guardians, and many teenagers under the age of 18 are also parents.

In 2009, the NSPCC conducted research with young people aged 13–17 in mainstream education which examined their experiences of physical, emotional and sexual forms of violence in their partner relationships. The research found that:

⇨ 25% of girls (the same proportion as for adult women) and 18% of boys experienced some form of physical abuse;

⇨ 75% of girls and 50% of boys reported some sort of emotional abuse; and

⇨ 33% of girls and 16% of boys reported some form of sexual abuse.

In addition, results showed that having an older partner, and in particular a 'much older' partner, was a significant risk factor for girls. Overall, three-quarters of girls surveyed with a 'much older' partner (which was defined by the girls participating as being more than two years older) had experienced some form of physical violence.

A second small-scale report by the NSPCC looked at violence in intimate relationships of disadvantaged teenagers who are not in mainstream education. Although the study does not claim to be representative of the UK population:

⇨ More than half of the girls who supplied information in the study said they had been in a sexually violent relationship before they were 18 and over half of the girls reported that they had been a victim of physical violence in at least one of their intimate relationships.

⇨ A quarter of boys who responded said they had dated physically aggressive partners.

We know that there is a stigma surrounding the issue of teenage relationship abuse. Young people may feel they are not taken seriously by adults, and research indicates that adults can trivialise abuse or minimise the effects of emotional abuse due to the lack of visible harm. Research has shown that young people are much more likely to disclose relationship abuse issues to a friend or peer than to a parent or social worker.

It is estimated that over 20,000 girls under the age of 15 in England and Wales are potentially at risk of female genital mutilation

---

The Government's teenage relationship abuse campaign was recently re-launched by the Home Office. The campaign ran from September to November 2011 and aimed to prevent teenagers from becoming victims and perpetrators of abusive relationships. The campaign encouraged teenagers to rethink their views of acceptable violence, abuse or controlling behaviour in relationships and directed them to places for help and advice.

The 'This is Abuse' website (thisisabuse.direct.gov. uk) gives teens the chance to discuss the issues with their peers and get access to third-party support and advice. We also ran online discussion forums during the campaign, with the support of our partners such as Against Violence and Abuse, Women's Aid, Respect, Men's Advice Line, Broken Rainbow and Beat Bullying.

To date there have been 151,998 visits to the This is Abuse website.

Forced marriage

Statistics from the Forced Marriage Unit (FMU) from January to December 2010 show:

⇨ over 1,700 instances where the FMU gave advice or support relating to a possible forced marriage were received;

⇨ 35% of the assistance cases involved minors (those under 18) and of that number almost 14% involved minors who were aged 16 and under;

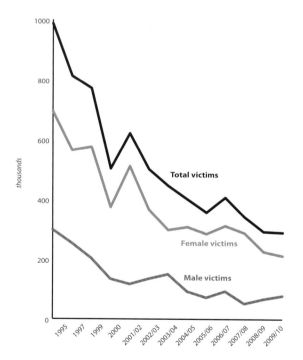

Estimated prevalence of incidents of domestic violence, England and Wales, 1995-2009/10.

Over the period, the proportions of male victims, based on the estimated numbers of incidents, has varied between 15% and 34%, with a mean of about 24%. Since male victims tend to suffer fewer repeat incidents against them than female victims, the proportions of actual male victims are higher than those based on the numbers of incidents shown on these figures. The more detailed BCS supplementary surveys specifically aimed at intimate violence detect much higher proportions of male victims, in the range of 35% to 50% for a last-year period.

Source: Government Statistics on Domestic Violence, *January 2011. (Dewar Research).*

HOME OFFICE

⇨ where the age was known, the oldest victim was 73 and the youngest was 12.

A forced marriage is a marriage in which one or both spouses do not (or, in the case of some vulnerable adults, cannot) consent to the marriage but are coerced into it. The key thing to focus on is choice – individuals should always be able to freely choose who they do or do not marry.

Forced marriage is a hidden practice, where due to its nature the full scale of the issue is unknown. It can happen to both men and women, although most cases involve young women and girls aged between 16 and 25.

The Unit provided direct support to victims in over 400 cases in the UK and to British nationals overseas. Around a third of assistance cases involved a minor (under 18 years old). The assistance provided ranged from simple advice, through to aiding a victim to prevent their unwanted spouse moving to the UK ('reluctant sponsor' cases), and, in extreme cases, the rescue of victims held against their will overseas.

Immigration

In relation to immigration, the UK Border Agency will not give permission to enter or remain in the UK to a person who is applying as a spouse/partner if they or their settled partner will be aged under 18 on the date when they would arrive in the UK or the date when permission to enter or remain would be given. There are provisions within the Immigration Rules (paragraph 289A) for victims of domestic violence who have entered as the spouse/partner of a settled person to apply for settled status (indefinite leave to remain).

Female genital mutilation (FGM)

FGM involves procedures that include the partial or total removal of the external female genital organs for non-medical reasons. Carrying out FGM is a crime in the UK. It is also an offence for UK nationals or permanent UK residents to carry out FGM abroad, or to aid, abet, counsel or procure the carrying out of FGM abroad, even in countries where the practice is legal.

FGM is recognised as a form of domestic violence and can also be recognised as a form of child abuse (depending on the age of the victim). It has serious health consequences, including the high risk of infection, long-term disability, severe problems in pregnancy and childbirth, and death.

It is estimated that over 20,000 girls under the age of 15 in England and Wales are potentially at risk of FGM.

The age at which girls undergo FGM varies enormously according to the community. The procedure may be carried out when the girl is newborn, during childhood or adolescence, just before marriage or during the first pregnancy. However, the majority of cases of FGM are thought to take place between the ages of five and eight and therefore girls within that age bracket are at a higher risk.

Children and domestic violence

Domestic violence affects both adults and children within the family. Some 200,000 children (1.8%) in England live in households where there is a known high risk of cases of domestic abuse or violence. Prolonged and/or regular exposure to domestic violence can have a serious impact on children's safety and welfare, despite the best efforts of parents to protect them. An analysis of Serious Case Reviews found evidence of past or present domestic violence in over half (53%) of cases. In addition, we know that children who are living in a home where domestic violence is occurring are often more likely to be subject to abuse themselves. Research shows that in between 30% and 66% of domestic violence cases, the abusive partner is also directly abusing children in the family. In addition, domestic violence often begins or increases during pregnancy. Any violence during pregnancy can affect not just the mother but also the unborn child. Indeed, domestic violence is known to be a major cause of miscarriage and stillbirth.

Statutory responsibilities for under-16s

Local Safeguarding Children's Boards (LSCBs) provide local guidance and procedures relating to children identified as 'at risk of significant harm'.

A local authority has a duty to safeguard and promote the welfare of children within their area who are in need (Section 17, Children Act 1989) and has a duty to investigate when there is reasonable cause to suspect that a child is suffering, or is likely to suffer, significant harm (Section 47, Children Act 1989).

If a child (someone under 18) is suffering significant harm as a result of abuse or neglect, they would come within the child protection framework and local authority responsibilities, which would be within the LSCB's remit.

Children who are subject to domestic violence are addressed in *Working Together to Safeguard Children – A guide to inter-agency working to safeguard and promote the welfare of children*, which recognises the need for professionals to safeguard children from harm arising from abuse or violence in their own relationships.

December 2011

⇨ The above information is an extract from the Home Office's *Cross-government definition of domestic violence, a consultation*, and is reprinted with permission. Visit www.homeoffice.gov.uk for more information on this and other related topics.

© Crown copyright

What to do if you are a victim of domestic violence

Domestic violence does not just mean that your partner is hitting you. The abuse can be psychological, physical, sexual or emotional.

Domestic violence can also include many things, such as the constant breaking of trust, psychological games, harassment and financial control. It is rarely a one-off incident and is usually a pattern of abuse and controlling behaviour.

It can affect adults in all types of relationships and can also involve violence between parents and children.

If you are in an abusive relationship, there are three important steps you must take:

⇨ recognise that it is happening to you;

⇨ accept that you are not to blame;

⇨ get help and support.

Lots of organisations can give you help and support, including Refuge and Women's Aid.

Getting help

This is perhaps the most important thing you can do.

In an emergency, call 999. Domestic violence is treated very seriously by the police, and they will take action to protect you. If it is not an emergency, you could contact your local police station and discuss your situation with them.

You can also contact independent organisations such as the National Domestic Violence Helpline or the Men's Advice Line to ask for help and advice.

The police will make sure that you get the help you need. They can put you in touch with volunteer organisations that provide refuge accommodation where you'll be safe.

Advice and support

There are many people and organisations you can turn to if you are suffering from domestic violence. Your GP, for example, can direct you to groups that work with victims of abuse. They can point you to local support groups and charities that help victims and their children escape the cycle of violence. They can make sure you find safe emergency refuge accommodation and put you in touch with people who can ensure that you're protected. You don't have to tell them your name. If you don't want to discuss it with your GP, you can call one of the helplines listed below.

⇨ English National Domestic Violence Helpline: 0808 2000 247.

⇨ Men's Advice Line: 0808 801 0327.

⇨ Wales Domestic Abuse Helpline: 0808 80 10 800.

⇨ Dyn Wales/Dyn Cymru (for men in Wales): 0808 801 0321.

⇨ Scottish Domestic Abuse Helpline: 0800 027 1234.

⇨ Northern Ireland Women's Aid 24-hour Domestic Violence Helpline: 0800 917 1414.

⇨ Broken Rainbow Helpline (for lesbian, gay, bisexual and transgender people): 0300 999 5428.

⇨ Respect Phoneline (for people who are abusive to partners and want help to stop): 0808 802 4040.

⇨ Forced Marriage Unit: 020 7088 0151.

Rights of domestic abuse victims

Children and your rights

Your abuser may threaten that if you leave or tell anyone about what's happening, your child will be taken away from you. it's important that you know that children's services will not take your child away for this reason.

If you fear your partner will abduct your children, get advice as soon as possible. Your local Women's Aid group, Refuge, Law Centre, Citizens' Advice Bureau or a solicitor can advise you on how to protect your child. They will explain how contact between your child and a violent partner can be restricted.

These groups will explain that, under the Family Law Act 1996, you can apply for an order that will protect you from threats or violence. This is called a 'non-molestation order'.

Your home and your rights

You can apply for an order that will protect your right to live safely in your family home (this is called an 'occupation order'). If granted, it could order your abuser to move out of the house, and forbid them even to enter it.

If you are in this situation please contact one of the advice groups.

⇨ Information from Directgov. Please visit www.direct.gov.uk for more information.

© Crown copyright

Domestic violence perpetrator programmes

Information from Respect.

Domestic violence perpetrator programmes are behaviour-change programmes run in small groups, aiming to:

➪ help men stop being violent and abusive;

➪ help them learn how to relate to their partners in a respectful and equal way;

➪ show them non-abusive ways of dealing with difficulties in their relationships and coping with their anger;

➪ keep their partner safer.

They run for several weeks and they meet once a week for about two and a half hours in the evening. They are not anger management classes.

A domestic violence perpetrator programme is the most appropriate type of help for men who are abusive and violent toward their partners. These programmes are also known as domestic violence prevention programmes (DVPP).

What happens at a domestic violence perpetrator programme meeting?

Some groups are discussion-based, but most use a variety of interactive exercises to make the learning realistic, stimulating and relevant to men's own situations. There are many different programmes across the UK, and the content will vary, but on the whole they will cover these issues:

What is violence and abuse? Why am I violent?

➪ Learning that I am in control of my own behaviour and can choose not to be violent.

➪ Taking responsibility for my behaviour, without blaming others or minimising it.

➪ Understanding the impact of violence and abuse on my partner and children.

➪ Learning how to notice when I am becoming abusive and how to stop.

➪ Learning different, non-abusive ways of dealing with difficulties in my relationship.

➪ Dealing non-abusively with my partner's anger.

➪ Negotiation and listening – how to build a respectful relationship.

How do domestic violence perpetrator programmes keep partners safe?

Every domestic violence perpetrator programme should have an attached service for partners offering information and support. In fact, a domestic violence perpetrator programme without such a service for the woman who has suffered the abuse is likely to increase the risks towards her rather than promote her safety.

Are there any domestic violence perpetrator programmes for women or for men in same-sex relationships?

Most domestic violence perpetrator programmes have been designed for men in heterosexual relationships. Some of these programmes also work with women (in heterosexual or same-sex relationships) and with gay/ bisexual men. For more information call the Respect Phoneline on 0808 802 4040.

➪ Information from Respect. Please visit www.respect. uk.net for more information.

© Respect

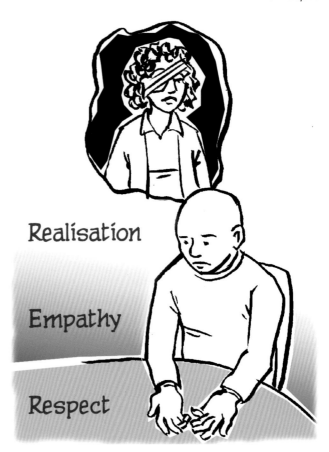

Realisation

Empathy

Respect

RESPECT

⇨ The Government defines domestic violence as: 'Any incident of physical, psychological or financial violence that takes place within an intimate or family-type relationship and that forms a pattern of coercive and controlling behaviour. This can include forced marriage and so-called 'honour crimes'. (page 1)

⇨ There is never an excuse for violence or abuse. Domestic violence is about power and control. (page 1)

⇨ More often than not men are the abusers and women are the victims, but domestic violence can also happen to men. (page 2)

⇨ 30% of domestic violence starts or worsens during pregnancy. (page 4)

⇨ Home Office figures reveal that on average, 100 women a year and around 30 men a year are killed within a domestic abuse context. Women are almost exclusively killed by men, whereas approximately one-third of the men are killed by other men. (page 5)

⇨ One in six men and one in four women will suffer domestic abuse in their lifetime. (page 11)

⇨ There are 72 bed spaces in 20 refuges or safe houses available for male victims in the UK. There are over an estimated 400 organisations, with 500 refuges (with 7,500 spaces) in the UK specifically for women. (page 11)

⇨ LGBT Youth Scotland and the Equality Network's 2010 examination of transgender people's experience of domestic abuse in Scotland found that 80% of respondents had experienced emotionally, sexually or physically abusive behaviour by a partner or ex-partner. (page 13)

⇨ Since 2004, people in LGBT relationships suffering domestic abuse have been equally protected by law in England, giving them the same rights as domestic violence victims in heterosexual relationships. (page 13)

⇨ The Forced Marriage Unit deals with about 400 cases of forced marriage every year, many of them involving minors. Around 15% of these cases involve boys and/or young men being forced to marry against their wishes. (page 15)

⇨ Risk factors which may increase a teenager's susceptibility to relationship abuse can include previous experiences of parental domestic violence, physical and sexual abuse and violent peer groups. (page 17)

⇨ Between July 2010 and June 2011, Parentline received 39,258 calls from parents experiencing physical or verbal aggression from their children. (page 22)

⇨ The estimated cost of domestic violence in England is £5.5 billion a year. This includes physical and mental health costs, criminal justice costs, social services costs, housing and refuge costs, civil legal costs and lost economic output. (page 27)

⇨ Up to three million women across the UK experience rape, domestic violence, forced marriage, stalking, sexual exploitation and trafficking, female genital mutilation (FGM) or so-called 'honour' violence each year. (page 28)

⇨ The British Crime Survey has found that women between 16 and 24 years of age and men aged between 16 and 34 years of age were more likely to suffer relationship abuse than any other age range. (page 34)

⇨ The 2009/10 British Crime Survey found 12.7% of women and 6.2% of men aged 16–19 had experienced some form of domestic abuse in the last year. (page 35)

⇨ Some 200,000 children (1.8%) in England live in households where there is a known high risk of cases of domestic abuse or violence. (page 37)

⇨ It is estimated that over 20,000 girls under the age of 15 in England and Wales are potentially at risk of female genital mutilation (FGM). (page 37)

Digital abuse

Most frequently occurring in teenage relationships, digital abuse involves the use of texting and social networking sites to keep track of, harass, stalk, control, bully or intimidate a partner.

Domestic abuse

Any incident of physical, sexual, emotional or financial abuse that takes place within an intimate partner relationship. Domestic abuse can be perpetrated by a spouse, partner or other family member and occurs regardless of gender, sex, race, class or religion.

Emotional abuse

Emotional abuse refers to a victim being verbally attacked, criticised and put down. Following frequent exposure to this abuse, the victim's mental wellbeing suffers as their self-esteem is destroyed and the perpetrator's control over them increases. They may suffer from feelings of worthlessness, believing that they deserve the abuse or that if they were to leave the abuser they would never find another partner. A victim way also have been convinced by their abuser that the abuse is their fault. The abuser can use these feelings to manipulate the victim.

Financial abuse

Financial, or economic, abuse involves controlling the victim's finances. This limits the victim's independence and ability to access help, and restricts their ability to leave the abusive relationship. Financial abuse can include withholding money or credit cards, exploiting mutual assets and forcing someone to quit their job or work against their will.

Forced marriage

A marriage that takes place without the consent of one or both parties. Forced marriage is not the same as arranged marriage, which is organised by family or friends but which both parties freely enter into.

'Honour' crime

An 'honour' crime or killing occurs when family members take action against a relative who is thought to have brought shame on the family. The victims are mostly women who are accused of dishonouring their family by going against their wishes (for example, by fleeing a forced marriage).

Perpetrator programme

A rehabilitation programme for perpetrators of domestic abuse which aims to help them understand and try to change their abusive behaviour.

Physical abuse

Physical abuse involves the use of violence or force against a victim and can including hitting, slapping, kicking, pushing, strangling or other forms of violence. Physical assault is a crime and the police have the power to protect victims, but in a domestic violence situation it can sometimes take a long time for the violence to come to light. Some victims are too afraid to go to the police, believe they can reform the abuse (who they may still love), or have normalised their abusive situation and do not realise they can get help.

Refuge

A shelter or safe house, offering a safe place for victims of domestic violence and their children to stay. Refuges can provide practical advice as well as emotional support for victims of domestic abuse until they can find somewhere more permanent to stay.

Sexual abuse

Sexual abuse occurs when a victim is forced into a sexual act against their will, through violence or intimidation. This can include rape. Sexual abuse is always a crime, no matter what the relationship is between the victim and perpetrator.

Stalking

Stalking is most frequently committed against women by former or current partners, although it can also be perpetrated by strangers or against men. The act of stalking usually involves obsessive, unwanted attention, and can sometimes escalate to violent or threatening behaviour.

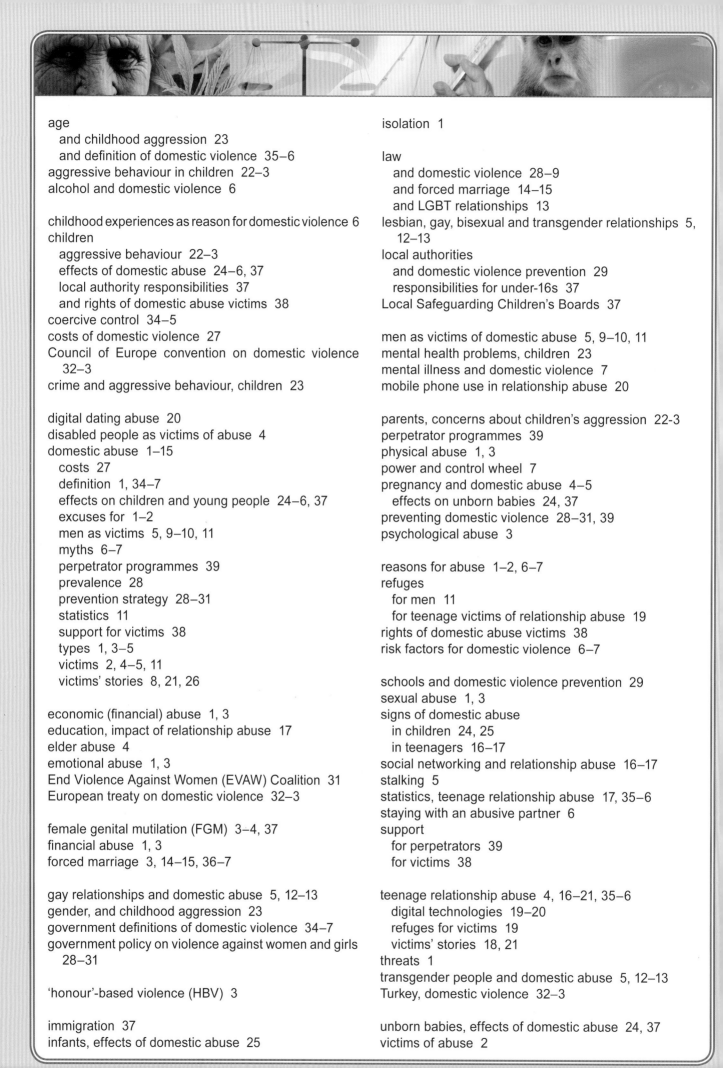

ACKNOWLEDGEMENTS

The publisher is grateful for permission to reproduce the following material.

While every care has been taken to trace and acknowledge copyright, the publisher tenders its apology for any accidental infringement or where copyright has proved untraceable. The publisher would be pleased to come to a suitable arrangement in any such case with the rightful owner.

Chapter One: Domestic Abuse

Domestic abuse, © Women's Aid, *Types of domestic abuse,* © NHS Barking and Dagenham 2012, Myths of domestic violence, © *Refuge,* Paula's story, © *Refuge,* The invisible domestic violence – against men, © *Guardian News & Media Ltd 2012,* Male victims of domestic and partner abuse, © *ManKind,* Understanding LGBT domestic abuse, © *Victim Support,* Out of sight, out of mind: transgender people's experience of domestic abuse, © *Victim Support,* What is forced marriage? © *ForcedMarriage.net,* Yasmin's story, © *ForcedMarriage.net*

Chapter Two: Young People and Abuse

What is teenage relationship abuse?, © Crown copyright is reproduced with the permission of Her Majesty's Stationery Office, *Key facts and statistics,* © Crown copyright is reproduced with the permission of Her Majesty's Stationery Office, *Plight of teens abused by violent lovers,* © 2011 Associated Newspapers Ltd, *Where are the refuges for teenagers in abused relationships?,* © Guardian News & Media Ltd 2011, *Digital abuse in teen relationships,* © loveisrespect. org, *Sophie's story,* © Women's Aid, *When family life hurts: family experience of aggression in children,* © Family Lives, *Effects of domestic abuse on children and young people,* © Welsh Women's Aid, *Sam's story,* © Refuge, T*eenage rape prevention,* © Crown copyright

is reproduced with the permission of Her Majesty's Stationery Office.

Chapter Three: Dealing with Abuse

Domestic violence costs £5.5 billion a year, © Trust for London, *A different world is possible,* © The End Violence Against Women Coalition, *UK must send a clear message on domestic violence,* © Guardian News & Media Ltd 2011, *What constitutes domestic abuse?,* © Crown copyright is reproduced with the permission of Her Majesty's Stationery Office, *What to do if you are a victim of domestic violence,* © Crown copyright is reproduced with the permission of Her Majesty's Stationery Office, *Domestic violence perpetrator programmes,* © Respect.

Illustrations

Pages 5, 20, 27, 36: Don Hatcher; pages 8, 21, 25, 33: Simon Kneebone; pages 11, 16, 23, 39: Angelo Madrid; pages 12, 30: Bev Aisbett.

Cover photography

Left: © Sanja Gjenero. Centre: © Miguel Ugalde. Right: © Dave Dyet.

Additional acknowledgements

Editorial on behalf of Independence Educational Publishers by Cara Acred.

With thanks to the Independence team: Mary Chapman, Sandra Dennis and Jan Sunderland.

Lisa Firth
Cambridge
April, 2012

The following tasks aim to help you think through the debate surrounding domestic abuse and provide a better understanding of the topic.

1 Brainstorm to find out what you know about domestic and relationship abuse. Who are the victims? Who are the perpetrators? What are the effects of domestic violence? Why do some people choose to abuse? Why do victims stay with abusive partners? When you have written down everything you can think of, come up with own definition of domestic abuse. Compare your list and definition with other students in your class.

2 Visit the Refuge website, www.refuge.org.uk. Write a report for your school newspaper explaining what Refuge do to help victims of domestic violence. Include case studies of survivors they have helped,

3 Read *Plight of teens abused by violent lovers* on page 18. Design a poster which could be displayed in schools and youth centres, helping teenagers to understand whether or not they are in an abusive relationship and where they can get help.

4 Imagine you have been asked to design a leaflet that will be made available in your local GP's surgery. The leaflet should explain the key facts about domestic and relationship abuse, as well as busting some of the myths surrounding it. Include a list of resources people can go to for information and support.

5 Why do you think domestic violence against male victims is under-reported? Discuss this with a partner. Make notes from your discussion and use these to construct a survey that will investigate people's views of men as victims of domestic abuse. When you have conducted your survey, write a report summarising your findings.

6 Write a blog post for a website that covers LGBT issues, on the subject of domestic abuse in same-sex relationships. Your post should highlight the similarities and differences between LGBT and heterosexual experiences of domestic violence.

7 Visit the Government's This is Abuse website at http://thisisabuse.direct.gov.uk and watch one of the 'If you could see yourself' videos. Do you think these are an effective way of encouraging teens to challenge sexually abusive behaviour? Storyboard your own anti-abuse video which could be used as part of the Government's campaign. It should be about 30 seconds long, the length of the average television advertisement.

8 Digital abuse in teenage relationships is an area of growing concern. Parents are often not fully aware of how this is perpetrated, or the effect it could have on their child. In groups, draw up plans for a smartphone app which would simulate digital dating abuse to help parents understand the issues.

9 Design a booklet aimed at teachers, outlining the warning signs that a pupil might be living in a household where domestic abuse is taking place. Consider both young children and teenagers.

10 Read *What constitutes domestic abuse?* on pages 34-37. Write a letter to your local MP, explaining which of the three options you support and why.

11 Write a diary entry from the viewpoint of a 15-year-old British girl whose family are trying to force her into marriage. Explore her emotions in this situation and the channels she might go through to seek help.

12 Read *Sam's story* on page 26. Create an illustrated picture book for the young children of domestic abuse survivors, helping them to understand and come to terms with their situation.

13 Read the song 'Make My Day' on page 31. Write your own song, rap or poem which challenges domestic violence.

14 Watch the film 'Sleeping with the Enemy', starring Julia Roberts. Write a review, focusing on the film's theme of domestic violence.

15 In pairs, role play a conversation between a woman who is being emotionally and physically abused by her partner and a concerned friend or family member. The family member is trying to convince the domestic violence victim to leave her abusive situation.

16 Imagine that you write an Agony Aunt column in a popular women's magazine. A reader has written to you explaining that she thinks she might be experiencing domestic abuse from her partner. The abuse is not physical but emotional. Write a reply, advising her on what steps she can take to leave the abusive situation.